SELECTED POEMS

WILLIAM COWPER was born in Hertfordshire in 1731. His mother died when he was six, and his childhood was often unhappy. After attending Westminster School he studied law. He was called to the Bar in 1754, subsequently becoming Commissioner of Bankrupts. In 1763, the prospect of a public examination for a post as Clerk of the Journals of the House of Lords triggered a serious mental breakdown. He spent eighteen months in an asylum, where in 1764 he experienced an Evangelical conversion. On leaving the asylum, Cowper went to live in Huntingdon, where he became friendly with Morley and Mary Unwin, an Evangelical couple. In 1767 Morley Unwin was killed in an accident, and Mary and Cowper moved to the small town of Olney in Buckinghamshire. Mary cared for him through recurrent bouts of depression, but when she died in 1796 his mental and physical health broke down. He died in 1800.

NICK RHODES was educated at the University of Manchester. He currently runs an international education services company and publishes Canto poetry CDs in association with Carcanet Press.

"stricken deer" 85 (19)

WILLIAM COWPER

Selected Poems

Edited with an introduction by
NICK RHODES

Fyfield*Books*

CARCANET

First published in Great Britain in 1984 by
Carcanet Press Limited
Alliance House
Cross Street
Manchester M2 7AQ

This impression 2003

A CIP catalogue record for this book is available from the British Library
ISBN 1 85754 712 8

The publisher acknowledges financial assistance from Arts Council England

Printed and bound in England by SRP Ltd, Exeter

CONTENTS

INTRODUCTION

WILLIAM COWPER was born on 15 November 1731 at the rectory house in Great Berkhamstead. His father, about whom we know very little, was Chaplain to George II. His mother, Ann Donne, who died when Cowper was only six years old, claimed to be descended from the poet John Donne and, further back, from Henry III. Cowper always felt a special affection for his mother, or at least for the idea of her, and as the years went by this feeling intensified. In 1790 he was sent her miniature from Norfolk. It inspired the poem 'On the Receipt of my Mother's Picture', an exquisite love poem, and one in which the form answers exactly to the natural rhythms of voice. It gives the impression of someone with an uncommonly acute sense of his meaning.

Soon after his mother's death, Cowper was sent to a boarding school in the nearby village of Market Street. It was a rough experience. One of the older boys picked him out and started to bully him. Cowper was terrified. In the end he knew his attacker better by the buckle on his shoe than by his face, and even after many years he was able to recall the whole affair in painful detail. We can only guess at the deeper effects. He remained throughout his life something of a natural victim, exceptionally raw-nerved and sensitive. Suffering was part of his nature, and might well have proved unbearable had it not discovered in him a certain acceptance and resilience.

Cowper's main schooling took place at Westminster, then one of the foremost public schools in England and generally regarded as the proper place for the sons of the ascendant Whig oligarchy. Cowper's father shared that view and rather hoped that his son would one day follow in the footsteps of his own uncle, the first Earl Cowper, who had served as Whig Chancellor under Anne and George I. Cowper did otherwise, of course, though his poems give ample evidence— even allowing for the attack on public schools in 'Tirocinium'—of the impact of this Whiggish-liberal, genteel education. We know too that he enjoyed and benefited from the companionship of his contemporaries, some of whom became outstanding figures in their day: George Colman, author of *The Jealous Wife*; Robert Lloyd, the poet, Warren Hastings; Bonnell Thornton; Sir William Russell; and Charles Churchill, the satirist, who had a marked influence on Cowper's early writing.

Westminster gave him another benefit: a thorough grounding in the classics. By the time he left school he could write almost as easily in Latin as he could in English. He had also gained enough confidence in his linguistic skills eventually to undertake large translation projects, including the verses of his old tutor Vincent Bourne, and, more grandly, the works of Homer. Homer took him a full six years, from 1784 to 1790, to complete, although for us now, looking back, while it certainly gave him some financial security and what was by then a much-needed routine of work, it appears largely as a wasted effort. Cowper has been accused in particular of failing to capture in his blank verse the vitality and martial stir of Homer's original— which is, unfortunately, hardly more read now than is Cowper's version of it.

At eighteen Cowper went off to be articled to a London solicitor called Mr Chapman at Ely Place, Holborn. It was not his choice. He went to please his father. For himself, though still rather in love with life, he nursed no strong ambition. Passive by nature, he remained throughout his life careless of the need to make his impact on the great world. In this respect, then, the Law was well-chosen. It was a singularly supportive profession, and it enabled one of Cowper's inclinations and background to make some sort of progress without much exertion. He took chambers in the Middle Temple and, in 1754, was called to the Bar. A year later he was admitted to the Inner Temple, and a year after that was appointed to the sinecure post of Commissioner of Bankrupts, with a stipend of £60 a year. Most of his time, however, was spent in other pursuits. He wrote verses, mainly imitations, but also two or three ballads which, he tells us, achieved some street popularity, but which have sadly been lost. There was also a series of poems addressed to 'Delia', or, in real

life, Theodora, his cousin. Cowper and she first met in 1750 at her ^{MB}
father's house in Southampton Row. They fell in love and were,
for the next few years, engaged to be married. However, it never
happened. For some reason—perhaps the blood-relationship, perhaps
Cowper's lack of certain prospects—Theodora's father opposed the
match and the affair petered out. Not that it seems to have been
much of a deprivation, at least not to Cowper. The poems, if poems
are evidence, lack depth of feeling. Their greatest virtue is an early
show of the technical deftness which distinguishes his later work.
But this, so early on, only seems to trivialize the 'thought'. James
Croft was right to suggest that the publication of apprenticework
adds nothing to the achievements of maturity. (1)

In general these early years were happy ones. Youth and its energies
prevailed. When he was not over in Southampton Row 'giggling and
making giggle', he would join in with the high-spirited carryings-on
of some of his ex-Westminster friends, who had formed a group called
the Nonsense Club, and who, among other things, contributed to
Colman's *Connoisseur*, one of several *Spectator*-like periodicals that
were around at the time. Cowper himself produced five papers for
it, and these show that had he wanted to he might well have done
something in the line of light-satirical prose. As it was, all his skills
and inclinations in that direction went into his private correspondence,
and for that we can be grateful. Cowper's letters are far more original
and compelling than any number of imitative essays could have been.
Their sustained elegance and their light-humoured depiction of
everyday human affections and events, however small and 'ordinary',
put them up amongst the very best letters in the language.

Cowper's *dilettante* life-style came to an end in 1763, when he
was thirty-two. It ended abruptly and dramatically, and is usually
taken to mark off the first period of his life. The second half could
hardly have been more different, spent at a remove from fashionable
society and clouded by a recurrent, at times raving, melancholia. As
to *why*—like so many of his contemporaries—Cowper should have
been thus afflicted, there is no clear explanation. All sorts of causes

9

have been cited: psychological, religious, neurological, physiological, even nutritional. But all we know for certain is what first triggered it: the threat of a public examination, as part of his proposed election to the post of Clerkship of the Journals in the House of Lords. The closer the examination loomed, the more frantic Cowper became. In the end he tried the escape of suicide, but failed—indeed he botched it rather badly—and soon afterwards he was confined to an asylum in St Albans.

Cowper was there for eighteen months, from the end of 1763 to June 1765, under the kindly regime of an Evangelical doctor called Nathanael Cotton. Recovery began, so the story goes, one morning in July 1764. Cowper emerged from a particularly pleasing dream and immediately picked up his Bible, starting to read from St Paul's Epistle to the Romans. Suddenly, for the first time in many months, he began to experience an in-rush of hope, an almost hysterical joy. This was, in true Evangelical tradition, the moment of his conversion, the turning-point in his life.

It is worth stressing, however, that this 'turning' was by no means from a life of utter irreligion—even though that is how Cowper himself saw it. After all, his father had been a man of the cloth, and there is no evidence to suggest that Cowper had ever done anything to disgrace him. But then the Evangelicals were partly defined by their opposition to the Anglican Establishment. That was the enemy, at least so far as it had grown increasingly rationalistic and 'enlightened' in its approach to doctrine, following closely the lines of Locke's and Toland's philosophies. To the Anglican Evangelicals this was anathema. They, and the thousands of others outside the parochial system, many of them new-industrial and agricultural workers galvanized into faith by the phenomenal zeal and oratory skills of Wesley and Whitefield, shared a common regard for religion as a matter of *urgency*. They insisted on the primary authority of Scripture read in a literal spirit. They stressed revelation and salvation and, above all, a continuing, personal relationship of each person with God. In short, their religion was largely an affair of the heart.

10

Much of what Cowper wrote was affected by these doctrines. In his own life, however, his grip on this new-won faith proved insecure. Aside from a few buoyant, devotional years, he spent most of his life in a state of severe internal conflict and doubt, suffering particularly from a conviction that he, uniquely among mankind, had been selected by God for an irrevocable, special damnation. In his worst moments, he believed that this judgement might come crashing down on him at any time. In 1773 the notions were fixed. He experienced an utterly devastating dream, 'before the recollection of which all consolation vanishes, and, it seems to me, must always vanish'. (2) Soon he was raving, had to be physically restrained or comforted like a child. Although eventually his wits returned, he never recovered his faith. Mention of religion was an acute torment, and he was unable to enter a church.

Would any of this have happened if Cowper had managed to evade the Calvinism of Whitfield, with its highly-charged doctrine of election, and found instead a vein of Wesley's more humane Universalism? It is a question often raised and possibly unanswerable; but however one addresses it, one must always be sure to consult the *poems*. In them, the qualities of emotional brightness and darkness are plainly not two sides of the same coin. In 'The Shrubbery' and 'The Castaway', for instance, as indeed in all those poems where suffering occurs as a main theme, little or nothing seems to emanate from dogma, not even from the peculiarly distorted dogma of Cowper's own conceiving. Instead, one gets the impression of a vague, fathomless passion. Religion provides metaphors, but the suffering comes from elsewhere, a deeper source, perhaps his obsessive sense of his isolation, which after all predated his conversion and in the end brushed aside all its good effects. One of the greatest ironies in our literary history is surely that this poet became the leading spokesman for the Religious Revival, admired as much for his humanitarianism and asceticism, as for the simple force of his faith.

Cowper quitted St Albans in 1765. He resigned his Commissionership and went to live in the sleepy town of Huntingdon, where he

11

remained for two years. During this time he met and established an intimacy with an Evangelical family called Unwin, and in particular with Mrs Unwin, who was to become a life-long companion. When her husband was killed in a riding accident in 1767, she and Cowper removed to the small linen-town of Olney, in Buckinghamshire, near the river Ouse.

They lived in a house called Orchard Side. It has since become the Cowper Museum, and it still gives a clear impression of the restrictedness and almost too-cosy domesticity of Cowper's years in the place. Here is where he kept his famous pet hares—Puss, Bess and Tiney—and where he gardened, wrote, and passed his peaceful evenings musing and chatting by the fireside. This is the quintessential image of Cowper, and it pervades his work with a vital and immediate presence.

Mary Unwin looked after him. She filled to a degree the gap left by his mother. For his stability of mind her constant cheeriness and practical good sense were of inestimable value. She was one of several people close to Cowper who provided him with suggestions for his poetry. She it was who proposed the theme of 'The Progress of Error', the first of what eventually became the eight *Moral Satires*, Cowper's first extended composition and one in which he chose to cut his teeth on Juvenalian satire, and on the closed couplet of Pope. (3) His intention was to outline and defend the major moral and doctrinal preoccupations of the Evangelical faith. In the event, the writing suffers from just that, too much *intention*, a parade of confused ideas and themes, which do not often enjoy the support of personal feeling. In Cowper's verse, this is fatal. One looks to him for a special tension of head and heart, not the pure twist of thought. Not that these poems are entirely without felt conviction. The account of the journey to Emmaus, for instance, evinces a genuine, suasive devotion, simply and with little violence of transformation borne across from its scriptural source. 'Retirement', too, contains much excellent writing. The last in the series, it shows Cowper arriving at a certain facility of writing. It is more sustained, more *poetical*, than the preceding verses, and suffers none of their occasional slight breathlessness and gnomic patness. Moreover, its natural descriptions foreshadow the major achievement of *The Task*.

The *Moral Satires* appeared in Cowper's first volume, in 1782. They were greeted with general, if not unmixed, approval. This was not the first time he had been in print. The *Olney Hymns* of 1879—the earliest properly organized hymnal in the language and something of a rallying-standard for the Revival—contained 66 hymns by Cowper. The others, all 282 of them, were the work of the Rev. John Newton, a notorious slave-trader turned Evangelical, the curate of Olney, and a potent (some would say oppressive) influence on Cowper's life. He could not have been more different in temperament from Cowper: energetic, purposeful, strong-willed and robust—characteristics which his hymns to a degree reflect. By contrast, Cowper's hymns are more tentative, the strains of anxiety mingling curiously with those of celebration. They are not, indeed, model hymns, nor yet are they quite devotional lyrics, though they possess something of that *genre*. They stand quite alone, extraordinary and moving instances of a trembling selfhood hazarded within a vigorously communal and stylized medium.

But this is the stamp of much of Cowper's poetry: an intensely personal note blending with a staunch conventionality. It is easy to overlook. In *The Task*, one is so aware of a certain inherent *slackness* in Cowper's muse, and of how well it responds to the freedoms of blank verse, that one tends to forget the very large number of poems in which this is simply not the case. It is most unusual: after all, the impulse to write about oneself, especially if that impulse is at all confiding and intimate, as Cowper's is, would seem of necessity— outside a formal age—to demand its own forms, new ones, certainly if it is to avoid the impression of *straining against* the form. But Cowper disproves this. Convention releases him. In poem after poem—'The Colubriad', 'John Gilpin', 'The Poplar Trees', 'Alexander Selkirk'—one finds him tackling an insistent rhythm, or form, or convention, with total ease. In a quite exceptional way, he satisfies all their initiatives, while at the same time transforming them into something wholly personal and spontaneous in effect.

13

In 1780, John Newton left Olney for London. It was no great loss: all Cowper's best poetry came later, and this leads one to suspect that, had he remained under Newton's eye, as he was when he wrote the *Olney Hymns* and the *Moral Satires* (to which Newton contributed the preface), he would never have broken away from the stricture to be *morally useful* in his art. In the early days this had been his own constant profession. But it had little to do with the mass of excellent comic verse he went on to write, and it had significantly faded from his correspondence by the time he got around to *The Task*, still a substantially purposive work, but one in which the door opened a little wider to the imagination, the natural curve of Cowper's creativity.

If the loss of John Newton's company was beneficial to Cowper, at least as far as the poetry was concerned, the loss, later on, of Mary Unwin destroyed him. 'To Mary' is an eloquent testimony to the tenderness of his feelings towards her. Like 'On the Receipt of my Mother's Picture', the sheer *integrity* of its emotion makes any charge of sentimentality quite absurd. Mary died in 1796, after a long and harrowing illness, and thus deprived Cowper of a life structure on which for more than thirty years he had been uncommonly dependent. Now the despair, which had long been with him, but which he had for the most part effectively suppressed, came flooding back, and in the last lines of 'The Castaway' found powerful expression. This poem confirms Cowper's mastery of narrative pace and cadence, and it has about it all the affirmation of a finely-wrought thing. As an event in Cowper's life, however, it represents a final collapse. He wrote no more original verse. After a period in which he whittled away at a revised version of his Homer, and at some translations of Gay's *Fables*, he died on 25 April 1800. He was buried in East Dereham Church, near Mary Unwin.

Biographies as short as this tend to simplify the story. Cowper's becomes a 'tragic' one. Yet, as far as his poems are concerned, that is not the impression at all. Collectively they present a body of work that is predominantly pleasurable, insistently life-drawn. Of dementia and hopelessness there is astonishingly little evidence. We must assume either that they were not 'suitable subjects', or that biography can never tell the whole story.

The fact is, Cowper *made* poems. They needed to be crafted, as did the furniture and bird-cages he made. To an extent, they all served the same purpose, taking his mind off the desolating thoughts which, in 'An Epistle to Robert Lloyd Esq.', he describes with a rather whimsical touch as 'fierce banditti',

> That, with a black infernal train
> Make cruel inroads in my brain,
> And daily threaten to drive thence
> My little garrison of sense.   (15-18)

But Cowper was also a man of his time. The construction of poems was still regarded as a highly *deliberate* act. It demanded a deference to audience, and also to hard rules, principally those of correctness, restraint and decorum. Poetry was, like all the arts, a form of pro-social behaviour, especially in its satirical vein. It faced society as it were from within. And from Cowper, 'retirement' or no, there were no exceptions. His poems are never indecorous. Even 'Lines Written during a Period of Insanity', for all its oneiric profusion of imagery, its hellish privacy, is careful enough to clothe the experiential horror in appropriate English Sapphics, and acquire the sanction of the manner of Isaac Watts (*cf.* 'The Day of Judgement'). It registers itself, in other words, as a piece of literature. It is not, in any useful sense, 'insane'. Nor does it pretend to be the naked language of the soul—though that may well be its impact.

Cowper never simply gives of himself. His work, though personal in flavour, is seldom very introspective or self-exploratory in the way of the Romantic individualists. He greatly impressed the young Wordsworth and Coleridge, of course. As 'transitional' poet he had

15

helped to pull English verse back from conventionalized self-portrayal and excessively 'literary' received experience. But he was no rebel. He had no desire to flout tradition. He did not sit down and say, 'I am going to make something new'. Simply the thing he was, made him write. His newness and originality were the products of his desire and unique ability to reconcile his own experience of life with his two great concerns—Calvinist Christianity and literature (as it was then perceived). The interplay of these elements, their harmonious confusion produced, then as now, an effect quite unlike anything else in English verse.

At times this effect can be very disturbing. Compare, for instance, 'On the Death of Mrs Throckmorton's Bulfinch' with Gray's 'Ode on the Death of a Favourite Cat'. Both are mock-heroic: grandiloquence applied to a humble subject. But where Gray's poem draws from this all the usual bathos and humour, Cowper's poem grows dark. Pity and horror invest his little narrative with an excess of force, and it hammers silently and violently against the absurdly fragile cage-bars of a jaunty, urbane rhetoric. Social behaviour is under strain, and one does not have to be excessively ingenious to see behind this shades of Cowper's own circumstances. Much the same could be said of 'Alexander Selkirk', a tale of isolation, or even of 'On the Loss of the Royal George', which on the surface looks like a perfectly straightforward, typically patriotic dirge, but in which the image of drowning at sea links our thoughts to Cowper's other uses of the image, denoting the engulfment of self. But in this direction one should tread carefully. These poems attain a balance of passion and skill which is both thrilling and exact. Too much 'psychology' can topple it all.

In this respect, *The Task* has suffered badly. The achievement of it, its essential displacement from the prevailing conditions of Cowper's life, have too often been overlooked in the telling of his story. Some of this, perhaps, can be put down to Cowper himself, to the way he uses language. He is so easy and digressive and vocative. He gives the impression of a poet simply spilling out the contents of his mind. Then, of course, those passages which have been couched in conspicuously *poetical* styles—Augustan-social, sub-Miltonic, mock-heroic, circumlocutive, and so on—seem merely spare and added on, like bits of icing. But the art conceals art. *All* his language is deliberate. It is as hard-won as the colloquial ease of Prior, whom he so admired. Cowper was a deeply serious artist. He was striving all along for a form of expression that was both plain and simple; plain with the kind of meaning that stares up from the page, and simple as the language of the Bible is simple. In a letter to William Unwin, written in 1782, he says: 'To make verse speak the language of prose, without being prosaic, to marshall the words of it in such an order, as they might naturally take in falling from the lips of an extemporary speaker, yet without meanness; harmoniously, elegantly, and without seeming to displace a syllable for the sake of rhyme, is one of the most arduous tasks a poet can undertake.' To John Newton the year before he had written: 'I am merry that I may decoy people into my company, and grave that they may be the better for it. . . . A poet in my circumstances has a difficult part to act . . .'.

—'A difficult part to act'. Of all these revealing statements, this is the most striking. It tells us that Cowper was capable of regarding writing as an act of *projection*, not in the conspicuous manner of Gray or Chatterton, perhaps, but nonetheless as a considered affectation. And this, of course, begins the process of constructing a poetic personality, a *persona*. Other things continue the process, many of them—in the case of *The Task*—classical in origin. The poet's retirement theme, for instance, his ideal rural retreat, has a long tradition behind it, evident in numerous poems of the seventeenth and eighteenth centuries (Dryden, Johnson, Pope, Pomfret), and going back to Horace on his Sabine farm, Virgil, and beyond. Virgilian too is the concern with practical husbandry as a proper subject for poetry, which is most noticeable in a description of how to grow cucumbers, in Book II (*The Garden*). Then there is the whole moral-didactic, natural-descriptive mode itself, which came down to Cowper through the works of Goldsmith, Young and Thomson, 'the English Virgil'.

17

The Task is a chamber of such echoes. Indeed, there are so many of then, so intricately interwoven and overlapped with Cowper's own circumstances and interests, that it is quite impossible to say where one begins and another ends.

Conventionality, however, seems to fall away when Cowper turns his attention to the natural world. He walks into it, as it were *in person*. He looks around at it with a whim and unerring instinct for what is characteristic and life-giving in the thing observed. In so doing, of course, he distances himself from the school of Pope, with its abstractions and generalizations, and the large, fashionable set-pieces of the Picturesque. His way of looking seems to be a wholly random one, a casual, loving glancing-around at the throng of everyday delights on nature's surface. There is no desire to reveal a rational God through his works. Nature in itself reveals nothing but itself: a place of quiet pleasure, harmonious and friendly to man, an extension of the poem's domestic paradise.

This much strikes anyone reading *The Task* for the first time, and it distinguishes the poem. What is not so obvious is its underlying *meaningfulness*. Descriptions which might at first seem to be merely decorative, as though the poet is simply out to enjoy himself and share that enjoyment, or perhaps sugar the pill of his more sombre moral reflections, actually carry beneath them, if taken collectively, intentions of very much the same kind of metaphorical weight that one finds in Pope's 'Windsor Forest'. There is one difference, however. In Cowper's poem the exclusivity of natural harmony and peace, the complete absence of storm (which Cowper several times depicts as a sign of God's anger) is made to reflect on the divine stability and sanctity, not of the State, as in Pope's poem, but of the individual. In this sense, Nature *does* signify. But it does so only within the poem. While Cowper insists that Nature's divine values are perceptible only to 'the mind that has been touch'd from heav'n' (V 796), that same mind is also the consciousness of the poem, and we can thus share its perceptions as readers, by virtue of symbolic association.

18

This is what *The Task* is *about*: the representation and commendation of the state of grace, reinforced by a tradition-informed opposition of town and country: 'God made the country, and man made the town' (I 749). The 'hero' of the poem, its unifying and organizing principle, is the solitary 'stricken deer' who has left the herd. All his delight in the countryside results from grace; all his moral assertions are directed by grace. As a character he exists entirely within the precincts of the poem. The sum of its parts equals the sum of his experience, and ultimately any symbolic power they attain devolves on him. *The Task* is a web of such relations: absence of turbulence being a sign of his virtue; Winter's secureness, whiteness and stillness being the condition of his spirit in this life, held in a kind of suspension, in anticipation of the next season, 'an eternal spring' (VI 770). And that is the climactic conclusion of the poem, its sublime vision of Heaven. From the beginning that is where 'all things tend' (VI 818). The thought itself moves, in a kind of gently developing, meandering stream of consciousness. Even Time, most obviously in the last three books (evening, morning, noon), proceeds to the point where the winter sun is at its zenith. Unlike Thomson's *The Seasons*, which is cyclical, *The Task* is linear and progressive. It tends forward to the life to come.

At this level, the poem can be regarded as a compressed account of the spiritual life of one man. Who that man is, or rather what he represents, is best summed up by a short character sketch based on St Paul, who is, significantly, held up by Cowper as an instructive model.

Would I describe a preacher, such as Paul,
Were he on earth, would hear, approve, and own—
Paul should himself direct me. I would trace
His master-strokes, and draw from his design.
I would express him simple, grave, sincere;
In doctrine uncorrupt; in language plain,
And plain in manner; decent, solemn, chaste,
And natural in gesture; much impress'd

Himself, as conscious of his awful charge,
And anxious mainly that the flock he feeds
May feel it too; affectionate in look,
And tender in address, as well becomes
A messenger of grace to guilty men.   (II 395-407)

This is the 'I' *persona* exactly, one purified by what he is, as much as
by what he says, into 'a messenger of grace to guilty men'. It is not
'Cowper'. He knew well enough what storms were about. *The Task*
fulfilled the aspirations of a faith that excluded him.

The poem came out in 1785. From modest beginnings—the simple
task of writing on the subject of a 'sofa' (the playful suggestion of his
friend Lady Austen)—it developed into something on a grand scale.
And it made Cowper famous. For more than a hundred years after
its appearance, Cowper was a household name, generally held to be
one of England's best poets. To some extent, this was bolstered by a
certain uncritical 'extra-literary' sympathy: his *themes* were popular.
And late Victorians were no less grateful than the early Revivalists
had been to find in him a writer of such probity-and-pleasure. But
this is not the whole story. Cowper is far more than an appealing
practical moralist, or a palatable expounder of doctrine. The tag
'poet of the Religious Revival' does no justice to the remarkable
versatility and sheer secular *aliveness* of his genius—'John Gilpin',
the charming animal fables, the great miscellany of light and 'occa-
sional' poems, and poems addressed to his friends. Even *The Task*,
the great centre-piece of his *oeuvre*, rises above particular doctrine,
above even the assertion of what is True, which when it features
at all is more often than not embedded in the depiction of the
real and its associated symbols. For us, as 'impartial' readers, by
far the strongest, most memorable impressions of *The Task*—and
this could be applied to almost any of Cowper's poems—are those
of a profound gratitude for the simpler moments in life, a longing
for stability and calm, and, above all, a belief in an absolute good-
ness. Such 'themes' are no more specific to Christians than to

20

anyone else. Nor do they go out of fashion. Cowper can still be read, and should be, and not least for his intense, rare humanity.

NOTES

1. James Croft, Theodora's nephew, published Cowper's *Early Poems* in 1825. He expressed his view in the preface.
2. Letter to John Newton, 16 October 1785.
3. 'Table Talk', 'The Progress of Error', 'Truth', 'Expostulation', 'Hope', 'Charity', 'Conversation', 'Retirement'.

SELECT BIBLIOGRAPHY

Texts

Milford, H. S. (ed.), *The Poetical Works of William Cowper*, 4th edition, with corrections and additions by Norma Russell (London, 1967)
Wright, Thomas (ed.), *The Correspondence of William Cowper*, 4 vols. (London, 1904)

Critical and Biographical Works

Bagehot, Walter, 'William Cowper', *National Review* (July 1855), republished in *Literary Studies* (London, 1879)
Cecil, David, *The Stricken Deer* (London, 1929)
Davie, Donald, 'The Critical Principles of William Cowper', *Cambridge Journal*, vol. 7, no. 3 (December 1953), pp. 182-8
Enright, D. J., 'William Cowper', in *From Dryden to Johnson*, The New Pelican Guide to English Literature vol. 4 (Harmondsworth, 1982)
Fausset, Hugh I'Anson, *William Cowper* (London, 1928)
Free, William Norris, *William Cowper* (New York, 1970)

21

Hartley, Lodwick, *William Cowper: The Continuing Revaluation* (Chapel Hill, 1960)

Hayley, William, *The Life and Letters of William Cowper*, 4 vols. (London, 1803-6)

Hazlitt, William, 'On Thomson and Cowper', *Lectures on the English Poets* (London, 1964, Everyman Library)

Huang, Roderick, *William Cowper: Nature Poet* (London, 1951)

Hutchings, Bill, *The Poetry of William Cowper* (London, 1983)

Newey, Vincent, *Cowper's Poetry: A Critical Study and Reassessment* (Liverpool, 1982)

Nicholson, Norman, *William Cowper* (London, 1951)

Quinlan, Maurice J., *William Cowper: A Critical Life* (Minneapolis, 1953)

Ryskamp, Charles, *William Cowper of the Inner Temple Esquire* (Cambridge, 1959)

Smith, Goldwin, *Cowper* (London, 1880)

Spacks, Patricia Meyer, *The Poetry of Vision: Five Eighteenth-Century Poets* (Cambridge, Mass., 1967) pp. 165-206

Thomas, Gilbert, *William Cowper and the Eighteenth Century* (London, 1935)

collector;
director of Frick, Morgan Library

ON THE RECEIPT OF MY MOTHER'S
PICTURE OUT OF NORFOLK
The Gift of my Cousin Ann Bodham, 1790

Oh, that those lips had language! Life has pass'd
With me but roughly since I heard thee last.
Those lips are thine—thy own sweet smiles I see,
The same that oft in childhood solaced me;
Voice only fails, else, how distinct they say,
'Grieve not, my child, chase all thy fears away!'
The meek intelligence of those dear eyes
(Blest be the art that can immortalize,
The art that baffles time's tyrannic claim
To quench it) here shines on me still the same.   10
    Faithful remembrancer of one so dear,
Oh welcome guest, though unexpected, here!
Who bidd'st me honour with an artless song,
Affectionate, a mother lost so long,
I will obey, not willingly alone,
But gladly, as the precept were her own;
And, while that face renews my filial grief,
Fancy shall weave a charm for my relief—
Shall steep me in Elysian reverie,
A momentary dream, that thou art she.   20
    My mother! when I learn'd that thou wast dead,
Say, wast thou conscious of the tears I shed?
Hover'd thy spirit o'er thy sorrowing son,
Wretch even then, life's journey just begun?
Perhaps thou gav'st me, though unseen, a kiss;
Perhaps a tear, if souls can weep in bliss—
Ah that maternal smile! it answers—Yes.
I heard the bell toll'd on thy burial day,
I saw the hearse that bore thee slow away,
And, turning from my nurs'ry window, drew   30

A long, long sigh, and wept a last adieu!
But was it such?—It was.—Where thou art gone
Adieus and farewells are a sound unknown.
May I but meet thee on that peaceful shore,
The parting sound shall pass my lips no more!
Thy maidens griev'd themselves at my concern,
Oft gave me promise of a quick return.
What ardently I wish'd, I long believ'd,
And, disappointed still, was still deceiv'd;
By disappointment every day beguil'd,   40
Dupe of *to-morrow* even from a child.
Thus many a sad to-morrow came and went,
Till, all my stock of infant sorrow spent,
I learn'd at last submission to my lot;
But, though I less deplor'd thee, ne'er forgot.

    Where once we dwelt our name is heard no more,
Children not thine have trod my nurs'ry floor;
And where the gard'ner Robin, day by day,
Drew me to school along the public way,
Delighted with my bauble coach, and wrapt   50
In scarlet mantle warm, and velvet capt,
'Tis now become a history little known,
That once we call'd the past'ral house our own.
Short-liv'd possession! but the record fair
That mem'ry keeps of all thy kindness there,
Still outlives many a storm that has effac'd
A thousand other themes less deeply trac'd.
Thy nightly visits to my chamber made,
That thou might'st know me safe and warmly laid;
Thy morning bounties ere I left my home,   60
The biscuit, or confectionary plum;
The fragrant waters on my cheeks bestow'd
By thy own hand, till fresh they shone and glow'd;
All this, and more endearing still than all,

24

Thy constant flow of love, that knew no fall,
Ne'er roughen'd by those cataracts and brakes
That humour interpos'd too often makes;
All this still legible in mem'ry's page,
And still to be so, to my latest age,
Adds joy to duty, makes me glad to pay   70
Such honours to thee as my numbers may;
Perhaps a frail memorial, but sincere,
Not scorn'd in heav'n, though little notic'd here.
    Could time, his flight revers'd, restore the hours,
When, playing with thy venture's tissued flow'rs,
The violet, the pink, and jessamine,
I prick'd them into paper with a pin,
(And thou wast happier than myself the while,
Would'st softly speak, and stroke my head and smile)
Could those few pleasant hours again appear,   80
Might one wish bring them, would I wish them here?
I would not trust my heart—the dear delight
Seems so to be desir'd, perhaps I might.—
But no—what here we call our life is such,
So little to be lov'd, and thou so much,
That I could ill requite thee to constrain
Thy unbound spirit into bonds again.
    Thou, as a gallant bark from Albion's coast
(The storms all weather'd and the ocean cross'd)
Shoots into port at some well-haven'd isle,   90
Where spices breathe and brighter seasons smile,
There sits quiescent on the floods that show
Her beauteous form reflected clear below,
While airs impregnated with incense play
Around her, fanning light her streamers gay;
So thou, with sails how swift! hast reach'd the shore
'Where tempests never beat nor billows roar,'
And thy lov'd consort on the dang'rous tide

25

Of life, long since, has anchor'd at thy side.
But me, scarce hoping to attain that rest,   100
Always from port withheld, always distress'd—
Me howling winds drive devious, tempest toss'd,
Sails ript, seams op'ning wide, and compass lost,
And day by day some current's thwarting force
Sets me more distant from a prosp'rous course.
But oh the thought, that thou art safe, and he!
That thought is joy, arrive what may to me.
My boast is not that I deduce my birth
From loins enthron'd, and rulers of the earth;
But higher far my proud pretensions rise—   110
The son of parents pass'd into the skies.
And now, farewell—time, unrevok'd, has run
His wonted course, yet what I wish'd is done.
By contemplation's help, not sought in vain,
I seem t' have liv'd my childhood o'er again;
To have renew'd the joys that once were mine,
Without the sin of violating thine:
And, while the wings of fancy still are free,
And I can view this mimic shew of thee,
Time has but half succeeded in his theft—   120
Thyself remov'd, thy power to sooth me left.

from CONVERSATION

It happen'd, on a solemn even-tide,
Soon after He that was our Surety died,
Two bosom friends, each pensively inclin'd,
The scene of all those sorrows left behind,
Sought their own village, busied as they went,
In musings worthy of the great event: 510

26

They spake of him they lov'd, of him whose life,
Though blameless, had incurr'd perpetual strife,
Whose deeds had left, in spite of hostile arts,
A deep memorial graven on their hearts.
The recollection, like a vein of ore,
The farther trac'd, enrich'd them still the more;
They thought him, and they justly thought him, one
Sent to do more than he appear'd t' have done;
T' exalt a people, and to place them high
Above all else, and wonder'd he should die.   520
Ere yet they brought their journey to an end,
A stranger join'd them, courteous as a friend,
And ask'd them, with a kind engaging air,
What their affliction was, and begg'd a share.
Inform'd, he gather'd up the broken thread,
And, truth and wisdom gracing all he said,
Explain'd, illustrated, and search'd so well,
The tender theme, on which they chose to dwell,
That reaching home, the night, they said, is near,
We must not now be parted, sojourn here—   530
The new acquaintance soon became a guest,
And made so welcome at their simple feast,
He bless'd the bread, but vanish'd at the word,
And left them all exclaiming, 'Twas the Lord!
Did not our hearts feel all he deign'd to say,
Did they not burn within us by the way?

from RETIREMENT

Op'ning the map of God's evasive plan,
We find a little isle, this life of man;
Eternity's unknown expanse appears
Circling around and limiting his years;   150

27

The busy race examine and explore
Each creek and cavern of the dang'rous shore,
With care collect what in their eyes excels,
Some shining pebbles, and some weeds and shells;
Thus laden, dream that they are rich and great,
And happiest he that groans beneath his weight:
The waves o'ertake them in their serious play,
And ev'ry hour sweeps multitudes away;
They shriek and sink, survivors start and weep,
Pursue their sport, and follow to the deep.   160
A few forsake the throng; with lifted eyes
Ask wealth of heav'n, and gain a real prize—
Truth, wisdom, grace, and peace like that above,
Seal'd with his signet whom they serve and love;
Scorn'd by the rest, with patient hope they wait
A kind release from their imperfect state,
And, unregretted, are soon snatch'd away
From scenes of sorrow into glorious day.
[. . .]

And thou, sad suff'rer under nameless ill,
That yields not to the touch of human skill,
Improve the kind occasion, understand
A Father's frown, and kiss his chast'ning hand:
To thee the day-spring and the blaze of noon,
The purple ev'ning and resplendent moon,
The stars that, sprinkled o'er the vault of night,
Seem drops descending in a show'r of light,   350
Shine not, or undesir'd and hated shine,
Seen through the medium of a cloud like thine:
Yet seek him, in his favour life is found,
All bliss beside—a shadow or a sound:
Then heav'n, eclips'd so long, and this dull earth,
Shall seem to start into a second birth;

Nature, assuming a more lovely face,
Borrowing a beauty from the works of grace,
Shall be despis'd and overlook'd no more,
Shall fill thee with delights unfelt before,   360
Impart to things inanimate a voice,
And bid her mountains and her hills rejoice;
The sound shall run along the winding vales,
And thou enjoy an Eden ere it fails.
    Ye groves (the statesman at his desk exclaims,
Sick of a thousand disappointed aims,)
My patrimonial treasure and my pride,
Beneath your shades your grey possessor hide,
Receive me languishing for that repose
The servant of the public never knows.   370
Ye saw me once (ah, those regretted days
When boyish innocence was all my praise!)
Hour after hour delightfully allot
To studies then familiar, since forgot,
And cultivate a taste for ancient song,
Catching its ardour as I mus'd along;
Nor seldom, as propitious heav'n might send,
What once I valued and could boast, a friend,
Were witnesses how cordially I press'd
His undissembling virtue to my breast;   380
Receive me now, not uncorrupt as then,
Nor guiltless of corrupting other men,
But vers'd in arts that, while they seem to stay
A falling empire, hasten its decay.
To the fair haven of my native home,
The wreck of what I was, fatigu'd, I come;
For once I can approve the patriot's voice,
And make the course he recommends my choice;
We meet at last in one sincere desire,
His wish and mine both prompt me to retire.   390

'Tis done—he steps into the welcome chaise,
Lolls at his ease behind four handsome bays,
That whirl away from business and debate
The disencumber'd Atlas of the state.
Ask not the boy, who when the breeze of morn
First shakes the glitt'ring drops from every thorn
Unfolds his flock, then under bank or bush
Sits linking cherry stones, or platting rush,
How fair is freedom?—he was always free:
To carve his rustic name upon a tree,   400
To snare the mole, or with ill-fashion'd hook,
To draw th' incautious minnow from the brook,
Are life's prime pleasures in his simple view,
His flock the chief concern he ever knew—
She shines but little in his heedless eyes,
The good we never miss we rarely prize:
But ask the noble drudge in state affairs,
Escap'd from office and its constant cares,
What charms he sees in freedom's smile express'd,
In freedom lost so long, now repossess'd;   410
The tongue whose strains were cogent as commands,
Rever'd at home, and felt in foreign lands,
Shall own itself a stamm'rer in that cause,
Or plead its silence as its best applause.
He knows indeed that, whether dress'd or rude,
Wild without art, or artfully subdu'd,
Nature in ev'ry form inspires delight,
But never mark'd her with so just a sight.
Her hedge-row shrubs, a variegated store,
With woodbine and wild roses mantled o'er,   420
Green balks and furrow'd lands, the stream that spreads
Its cooling vapour o'er the dewy meads,
Downs that almost escape th' inquiring eye,
That melt and fade into the distant sky,

Beauties he lately slighted as he pass'd,
Seem all created since he travell'd last.
Master of all th' enjoyments he design'd,
No rough annoyance rankling in his mind,
What early philosophic hours he keeps,
How regular his meals, how sound he sleeps!   430
Not sounder he that on the mainmast head,
While morning kindles with a windy red,
Begins a long look-out for distant land,
Nor quits, till ev'ning watch, his giddy stand,
Then swift descending with a seaman's haste,
Slips to his hammock, and forgets the blast.
He chooses company, but not the squire's,
Whose wit is rudeness, whose good breeding tires;
Nor yet the parson's, who would gladly come,
Obsequious when abroad, though proud at home;   440
Nor can he much affect the neighb'ring peer,
Whose toe of emulation treads too near;
But wisely seeks a more convenient friend,
With whom, dismissing forms, he may unbend!
A man whom marks of condescending grace
Teach, while they flatter him, his proper place:
Who comes when call'd, and at a word withdraws,
Speaks with reserve, and listens with applause;
Some plain mechanic who, without pretence
To birth or wit, nor gives nor takes offence;   450
On whom he rests well-pleas'd his weary pow'rs,
And talks and laughs away his vacant hours.
The tide of life, swift always in its course,
May run in cities with a brisker force,
But no where with a current so serene,
Or half so clear, as in the rural scene.
Yet how fallacious is all earthly bliss,
What obvious truths the wisest heads may miss;

Some pleasures live a month, and some a year,
But short the date of all we gather here;   460
No happiness is felt, except the true,
That does not charm the more for being new.
This observation, as it chanc'd, not made,
Or if the thought occurr'd, not duly weigh'd,
He sighs—for, after all, by slow degrees,
The spot he lov'd has lost the pow'r to please;
To cross his ambling pony day by day,
Seems at the best but dreaming life away;
The prospect, such as might enchant despair,
He views it not, or sees no beauty there;   470
With aching heart, and discontented looks,
Returns at noon to billiards or to books,
But feels, while grasping at his faded joys,
A secret thirst of his renounc'd employs.
He chides the tardiness of ev'ry post,
Pants to be told the battles won or lost,
Blames his own indolence, observes, though late,
'Tis criminal to leave a sinking state,
Flies to the levee, and, receiv'd with grace,
Kneels, kisses hands, and shines again in place.   480

I. *Walking with God* Gen. v.24

Oh! for a closer walk with God,
　　A calm and heav'nly frame;
A light to shine upon the road
　　That leads me to the Lamb!

Where is the blessedness I knew
　　When first I saw the Lord?
Where is the soul-refreshing view
　　Of Jesus, and his word?　　　　　　　　　　8

What peaceful hours I once enjoy'd!
　　How sweet their mem'ry still!
But they have left an aching void,
　　The world can never fill.

Return, O holy Dove, return,
　　Sweet messenger of rest;
I hate the sins that made thee mourn,
　　And drove thee from my breast.　　　　　16

The dearest idol I have known,
　　Whate'er that idol be;
Help me to tear it from thy throne,
　　And worship only thee.

So shall my walk be close with God,
　　Calm and serene my frame;
So purer light shall mark the road
　　That leads me to the Lamb.　　　　　　　24

XXXV. *Light Shining out of Darkness*

God moves in a mysterious way,
    His wonders to perform;
He plants his footstep in the sea,
    And rides upon the storm.

Deep in unfathomable mines
    Of never failing skill;
He treasures up his bright designs,
    And works his sovereign will.   8

Ye fearful saints fresh courage take,
    The clouds ye so much dread
Are big with mercy, and shall break
    In blessings on your head.

Judge not the Lord by feeble sense,
    But trust him for his grace;
Behind a frowning providence,
    He hides a smiling face.   16

His purposes will ripen fast,
    Unfolding ev'ry hour
The bud may have a bitter taste,
    But sweet will be the flow'r.

Blind unbelief is sure to err,
    And scan his work in vain;
God is his own interpreter,
    And he will make it plain.   24

IX. *The Contrite Heart* Isa. lvii.15

The Lord will happiness divine
    On contrite hearts bestow:
Then tell me, gracious God, is mine
    A contrite heart, or no?

I hear, but seem to hear in vain,
    Insensible as steel;
If ought is felt, 'tis only pain,
    To find I cannot feel.   8

I sometimes think myself inclin'd
    To love thee, if I could;
But often feel another mind,
    Averse to all that's good.

My best desires are faint and few,
    I fain would strive for more;
But when I cry, 'My strength renew,'
    Seem weaker than before.   16

Thy saints are comforted I know,
    And love thy house of pray'r;
I therefore go where others go,
    But find no comfort there.

Oh make this heart rejoice, or ache;
    Decide this doubt for me;
And if it be not broken, break,
    And heal it, if it be.   24

XXXII. *The Shining Light*

My former hopes are fled,
My terror now begins;
I feel, alas, that I am dead
In trespasses and sins.

Ah, whither shall I fly?
I hear the thunder roar;
The law proclaims destruction nigh,
And vengeance at the door.   8

When I review my ways,
I dread impending doom;
But sure, a friendly whisper says,
'Flee from the wrath to come.'

I see, or think I see,
A glimm'ring from afar;
A beam of day that shines for me,
To save me from despair.   16

Fore-runner of the sun,
It marks the Pilgrim's way;
I'll gaze upon it while I run
And watch the rising day.

5|17|09

LINES WRITTEN DURING A PERIOD OF INSANITY (1774)

Hatred and vengeance, my eternal portion,
Scarce can endure delay of execution,
Wait, with impatient readiness, to seize my
                         Soul in a moment.

Damn'd below Judas: more abhorr'd than he was,
Who for a few pence sold his holy Master.
Twice betrayed Jesus me, the last delinquent,
                Deems the profanest.   8

Man disavows, and Deity disowns me:
Hell might afford my miseries a shelter;
Therefore hell keeps her ever hungry mouths all
                Bolted against me.

Hard lot! encompass'd with a thousand dangers;
Weary, faint, trembling with a thousand terrors;
I'm called, if vanquish'd, to receive a sentence
                Worse than Abiram's.   16

Him the vindictive rod of angry justice
Sent quick and howling to the centre headlong;
I, fed with judgment, in a fleshly tomb, am
                Buried above ground.

THE SHRUBBERY (1773)
Written in a Time of Affliction

Oh, happy shades—to me unblest!
    Friendly to peace, but not to me!
How ill the scene that offers rest,
    And heart that cannot rest, agree!

This glassy stream, that spreading pine,
    Those alders quiv'ring to the breeze,
Might sooth a soul less hurt than mine,
    And please, if any thing could please.   8

But fix'd unalterable care
   Foregoes not what she feels within,
Shows the same sadness ev'ry where,
   And slights the season and the scene.

For all that pleas'd in wood and lawn,
   While peace possess'd these silent bow'rs,
Her animating smile withdrawn,
   Has lost its beauties and its pow'rs.   16

The saint or moralist should tread
   This moss-grown alley, musing, slow;
They seek, like me, the secret shade,
   But not, like me, to nourish woe!

Me fruitful scenes and prospects waste
   Alike admonish not to roam;
These tell me of enjoyments past,
   And those of sorrows yet to come.   24

VERSES SUPPOSED TO BE WRITTEN BY ALEXANDER SELKIRK, DURING HIS SOLITARY ABODE IN THE ISLAND OF JUAN FERNANDEZ (1782)

I am monarch of all I survey,
   My right there is none to dispute;
From the centre all round to the sea,
   I am lord of the fowl and the brute.
Oh, solitude! where are the charms
   That sages have seen in thy face?
Better dwell in the midst of alarms,
   Than reign in this horrible place.   8

I am out of humanity's reach,
   I must finish my journey alone,
Never hear the sweet music of speech;
   I start at the sound of my own.
The beasts, that roam over the plain,
   My form with indifference see;
They are so unacquainted with man,
   Their tameness is shocking to me.   16

Society, friendship, and love,
   Divinely bestow'd upon man,
Oh, had I the wings of a dove,
   How soon would I taste you again!
My sorrows I then might assuage
   In the ways of religion and truth,
Might learn from the wisdom of age,
   And be cheer'd by the sallies of youth.   24

Religion! what treasure untold
   Resides in that heavenly word!
More precious than silver and gold,
   Or all that this earth can afford.
But the sound of the church-going bell
   These vallies and rocks never heard,
Ne'er sighed at the sound of a knell,
   Or smil'd when a sabbath appear'd.   32

Ye winds, that have made me your sport,
   Convey to this desolate shore
Some cordial endearing report
   Of a land I shall visit no more.
My friends, do they now and then send
   A wish or a thought after me?
O tell me I yet have a friend,
   Though a friend I am never to see.   40

How fleet is a glance of the mind!
    Compar'd with the speed of its flight,
The tempest itself lags behind,
    And the swift wing'd arrows of light.
When I think of my own native land,
    In a moment I seem to be there;
But alas! recollection at hand
    Soon hurries me back to despair.   48

But the sea-fowl is gone to her nest,
    The beast is laid down in his lair,
Ev'n here is a season of rest,
    And I to my cabin repair.
There is mercy in every place;
    And mercy, encouraging thought!
Gives even affliction a grace,
    And reconciles man to his lot.   56

ON THE LOSS OF THE ROYAL GEORGE (1782-3)
Written when the News Arrived

    Toll for the brave—
The brave! that are no more:
    All sunk beneath the wave,
Fast by their native shore.
    Eight hundred of the brave,
Whose courage well was tried,
    Had made the vessel heel
And laid her on her side
    A land-breeze shook the shrouds,
And she was overset;
    Down went the Royal George,
With all her crew complete.   12

Toll for the brave—
Brave Kempenfelt is gone,
　His last sea-fight is fought,
His work of glory done.
　It was not in the battle,
No tempest gave the shock,
　She sprang no fatal leak,
She ran upon no rock;
　His sword was in the sheath,
His fingers held the pen,
　When Kempenfelt went down
With twice four hundred men.　　　　　　　24

Weigh the vessel up,
Once dreaded by our foes,
　And mingle with your cup
The tears that England owes;
　Her timbers yet are sound,
And she may float again,
　Full charg'd with England's thunder,
And plough the distant main;
　But Kempenfelt is gone,
His victories are o'er;
　And he and his Eight hundred
Must plough the wave no more.　　　　　　36

THE DIVERTING HISTORY OF JOHN GILPEN (1782)
*Showing how he went farther than he intended,
and came home safe again.*

John Gilpin was a citizen
　Of credit and renown,
A train-band captain eke was he
　Of famous London town.

John Gilpin's spouse said to her dear—
    Though wedded we have been
These twice ten tedious years, yet we
    No holiday have seen.   8

To-morrow is our wedding-day,
    And we will then repair
Unto the Bell at Edmonton
    All in a chaise and pair.

My sister, and my sister's child,
    Myself, and children three,
Will fill the chaise; so you must ride
    On horseback after we.   16

He soon replied—I do admire
    Of womankind but one,
And you are she, my dearest dear,
    Therefore it shall be done.

I am a linen-draper bold,
    As all the world doth know,
And my good friend the calender
    Will lend his horse to go.   24

Quoth Mrs Gilpin—That's well said;
    And, for that wine is dear,
We will be furnish'd with our own,
    Which is both bright and clear.

John Gilpin kiss'd his loving wife;
    O'erjoy'd was he to find
That, though on pleasure she was bent,
    She had a frugal mind.   32

The morning came, the chaise was brought,
    But yet was not allow'd
To drive up to the door, lest all
    Should say that she was proud.

So three doors off the chaise was stay'd,
    Where they did all get in;
Six precious souls, and all agog
    To dash through thick and thin!   40

Smack went the whip, round went the wheels,
    Were never folk so glad,
The stones did rattle underneath,
    As if Cheapside were mad.

John Gilpin at his horse's side
    Seiz'd fast the flowing mane,
And up he got, in haste to ride,
    But soon came down again;   48

For saddle-tree scarce reach'd had he,
    His journey to begin,
When, turning round his head, he saw
    Three customers come in.

So down he came; for loss of time,
    Although it griev'd him sore,
Yet loss of pence, full well he knew,
    Would trouble him much more.   56

'Twas long before the customers
    Were suited to their minds,
When Betty screaming came down stairs—
    'The wine is left behind!'

Good lack! quoth he—yet bring it me,
    My leathern belt likewise,
In which I bear my trusty sword
    When I do exercise.   64

Now mistress Gilpin (careful soul!)
    Had two stone bottles found,
To hold the liquor that she lov'd,
    And keep it safe and sound.

Each bottle had a curling ear,
    Through which the belt he drew,
And hung a bottle on each side,
    To make his balance true.   72

Then, over all, that he might be
    Equipp'd from top to toe,
His long red cloak, well brush'd and neat,
    He manfully did throw.

Now see him mounted once again
    Upon his nimble steed,
Full slowly pacing o'er the stones,
    With caution and good heed!   80

But, finding soon a smoother road
    Beneath his well-shod feet,
The snorting beast began to trot,
    Which gall'd him in his seat.

So, Fair and softly, John he cried,
    But John he cried in vain;
That trot became a gallop soon,
    In spite of curb and rein.   88

So stooping down, as needs he must
    Who cannot sit upright,
He grasp'd the mane with both his hands,
    And eke with all his might.

His horse, who never in that sort
    Had handled been before,
What thing upon his back had got
    Did wonder more and more.   96

Away went Gilpin, neck or nought;
    Away went hat and wig!—
He little dreamt, when he set out,
    Of running such a rig!

The wind did blow, the cloak did fly,
    Like streamer long and gay,
Till, loop and button failing both,
    At last it flew away.   104

Then might all people well discern
    The bottles he had slung;
A bottle swinging at each side,
    As hath been said or sung.

The dogs did bark, the children scream'd,
    Up flew the windows all;
And ev'ry soul cried out—Well done!
    As loud as he could bawl.   112

Away went Gilpin—who but he?
    His fame soon spread around—
He carries weight! he rides a race!
    'Tis for a thousand pound!

And still, as fast as he drew near,
    'Twas wonderful to view
How in a trice the turnpike-men
    Their gates wide open threw.   120

And now as he went bowing down
    His reeking head full low,
The bottles twain behind his back
    Were shattered at a blow.

Down ran the wine into the road,
    Most piteous to be seen,
Which made his horse's flanks to smoke
    As they had basted been.   128

But still he seem'd to carry weight,
    With leathern girdle brac'd;
For all might see the bottle-necks
    Still dangling at his waist.

Thus all through merry Islington
    These gambols he did play,
And till he came unto the Wash
    Of Edmonton so gay.   136

And there he threw the wash about
    On both sides of the way,
Just like unto a trundling mop,
    Or a wild goose at play.

At Edmonton his loving wife
    From the balcony spied
Her tender husband, wond'ring much
    To see how he did ride.   144

Stop, stop, John Gilpin!—Here's the house—
    They all at once did cry;
The dinner waits, and we are tir'd:
    Said Gilpin—So am I!

But yet his horse was not a whit
    Inclin'd to tarry there.
For why?—his owner had a house
    Full ten miles off, at Ware.   152

So like an arrow swift he flew,
    Shot by an archer strong;
So did he fly—which brings me to
    The middle of my song.

Away went Gilpin, out of breath,
    And sore against his will,
Till at his friend the calender's
    His horse at last stood still.   160

The calender, amaz'd to see
    His neighbour in such trim,
Laid down his pipe, flew to the gate,
    And thus accosted him:—

What news? what news? your tidings tell;
    Tell me you must and shall—
Say why bare-headed you are come,
    Or why you come at all?   168

Now Gilpin had a pleasant wit,
    And lov'd a timely joke;
And thus unto the calender
    In merry guise he spoke.

I came because your horse would come;
   And, if I well forebode,
My hat and wig will soon be here—
   They are upon the road.   176

The calender, right glad to find
   His friend in merry pin,
Return'd him not a single word,
   But to the house went in;

Whence straight he came with hat and wig;
   A wig that flow'd behind,
A hat not much the worse for wear,
   Each comely in its kind.   184

He held them up, and, in his turn,
   Thus show'd his ready wit—
My head is twice as big as your's,
   They therefore needs must fit.

But let me scrape the dirt away
   That hangs upon your face;
And stop and eat, for well you may
   Be in a hungry case.   192

Said John—It is my wedding-day,
   And all the world would stare,
If wife should dine at Edmonton
   And I should dine at Ware!

So turning to his horse, he said—
   I am in haste to dine;
'Twas for your pleasure you came here,
   You shall go back for mine.   200

Ah, luckless speech, and bootless boast!
    For which he paid full dear;
For, while he spake, a braying ass
    Did sing most loud and clear

Whereat his horse did snort, as he
    Had heard a lion roar,
And gallop'd off with all his might,
    As he had done before.   208

Away went Gilpin, and away
    Went Gilpin's hat and wig!
He lost them sooner than at first—
    For why?—they were too big!

Now, mistress Gilpin, when she saw
    Her husband posting down
Into the country far away,
    She pull'd out half a crown;   216

And thus unto the youth she said
    That drove them to the Bell—
This shall be yours when you bring back
    My husband safe and well.

The youth did ride, and soon did meet
    John coming back amain;
Whom in a trice he tried to stop,
    By catching at his rein;   224

But, not performing what he meant,
    And gladly would have done,
The frighted steed he frighted more,
    And made him faster run.

Away went Gilpin, and away
    Went post-boy at his heels!—
The post-boy's horse right glad to miss
    The lumb'ring of the wheels.   232

Six gentlemen upon the road,
    Thus seeing Gilpin fly,
With post-boy scamp'ring in the rear,
    They rais'd the hue and cry:

Stop thief! stop thief!—a highwayman!
    Not one of them was mute;
And all and each that pass'd that way
    Did join in the pursuit.   240

And now the turnpike gates again
    Flew open in short space;
The toll-men thinking, as before,
    That Gilpin rode a race.

And so he did—and won it too!—
    For he got first to town;
Nor stopp'd till where he had got up
    He did again get down.   248

Now let us sing—Long live the king,
    And Gilpin long live he;
And, when he next doth ride abroad,
    May I be there to see!

ON THE DEATH OF MRS THROCKMORTON'S BULFINCH (1788)

Ye nymphs! if e'er your eyes were red
With tears o'er hapless fav'rites shed,
   O share Maria's grief!
Her fav'rite, even in his cage,
(What will not hunger's cruel rage?)
   Assassin'd by a thief.   6

Where Rhenus strays his vines among,
The egg was laid from which he sprung,
   And though by nature mute,
Or only with a whistle blest,
Well-taught, he all the sounds express'd
   Of flagelet or flute.   12

The honours of his ebon poll
Were brighter than the sleekest mole;
   His bosom of the hue
With which Aurora decks the skies,
When piping winds shall soon arise
   To sweep up all the dew.   18

Above, below, in all the house,
Dire foe, alike to bird and mouse,
   No cat had leave to dwell;
And Bully's cage supported stood,
On props of smoothest-shaven wood,
   Large-built and lattic'd well.   24

Well-lattic'd—but the grate, alas!
Not rough with wire of steel or brass,
   For Bully's plumage sake,
But smooth with wands from Ouse's side,

With which, when neatly peel'd and dried,
    The swains their baskets make.   30

Night veil'd the pole—all seem'd secure—
When led by instinct sharp and sure,
    Subsistence to provide,
A beast forth sallied on the scout,
Long-back'd, long-tail'd, with whisker'd snout,
    And badger-colour'd hide.   36

He, ent'ring at the study door,
Its ample area 'gan to explore;
    And something in the wind
Conjectur'd, sniffing round and round,
Better than all the books he found,
    Food, chiefly, for the mind.   42

Just then, by adverse fate impress'd,
A dream disturb'd poor Bully's rest;
    In sleep he seem'd to view
A rat, fast-clinging to the cage,
And, screaming at the sad presage,
    Awoke and found it true.   48

For, aided both by ear and scent,
Right to his mark the monster went—
    Ah, Muse! forbear to speak
Minute the horrors that ensued;
His teeth were strong, the cage was wood—
    He left poor Bully's beak.

He left it—but he should have ta'en
That beak, when issued many a strain
    Of such mellifluous tone,

Might have repaid him well, I wote,
For silencing so sweet a throat,
    Fast set within his own.   60

Maria weeps—The Muses mourn—
So, when by Bacchanalians torn,
    On Thracian Hebrus' side
The tree-enchanter Orpheus fell;
His head alone remain'd to tell
    The cruel death he died.   66

THE NEEDLESS ALARM (1791)
A Tale

There is a field through which I often pass,
Thick overspread with moss and silky grass,
Adjoining close to Kilwick's echoing wood,
Where oft the bitch-fox hides her hapless brood,
Reserv'd to solace many a neighb'ring squire,
That he may follow them through brake and briar,
Contusion hazarding of neck and spine,
Which rural gentlemen call sport divine.
A narrow brook, by rushy banks conceal'd,
Runs in a bottom, and divides the field;   10
Oaks intersperse it, that had once a head,
But now wear crests of oven-wood instead;
And where the land slopes to its wat'ry bourn,
Wide yawns a gulph beside a ragged thorn;
Bricks line the sides, but shiver'd long ago,
And horrid brambles intertwine below;
A hollow scoop'd, I judge in ancient time,
For baking earth, or burning rock to lime.

53

Not yet the hawthorn bore her berries red,
With which the fieldfare, wint'ry guest, is fed;   20
Nor autumn yet had brush'd from ev'ry spray,
With her chill hand, the mellow leaves away;
But corn was hous'd, and beans were in the stack,
Now, therefore, issued forth the spotted pack,
With tails high mounted, ears hung low, and throats
With a whole gamut fill'd of heav'nly notes,
For which, alas! my destiny severe,
Though ears she gave me two, gave me no ear.
The sun accomplishing his early march,
His lamp now planted on heav'n's topmost arch,   30
When, exercise and air my only aim,
And heedless whither, to that field I came,
Ere yet with ruthless joy the happy hound
Told hill and dale that Reynard's track was found,
Or with the high-rais'd horn's melodious clang
All Kilwick and all Dingle-derry rang.
Sheep graz'd the field; some with soft bosom press'd
The herb as soft, while nibbling stray'd the rest;
Nor noise was heard but of the hasty brook,
Struggling, detain'd in many a pretty nook.   40
All seem'd so peaceful, that from them convey'd
To me, their peace by kind contagion spread.
But when the huntsman, with distended cheek,
'Gan make his instrument of music speak,
And from within the wood that crash was heard,
Though not a hound from whom it burst appear'd,
The sheep recumbent, and the sheep that graz'd,
All huddling into phalanx, stood and gaz'd,
Admiring, terrified the novel strain,
Then cours'd the field around, and cours'd it round again;   50
But, recollecting with a sudden thought,
That flight in circles urg'd advanc'd them nought,

They gather'd close around the old pit's brink,
And thought again—but knew not what to think.
   The man of solitude accustom'd long
Perceives in ev'ry thing that lives a tongue;
Not animals alone, but shrubs and trees,
Have speech for him, and understood with ease;
After long drought, when rains abundant fall,
He hears the herbs and flow'rs rejoicing all;   60
Knows what the freshness of their hue implies,
How glad they catch the largess of the skies,
But, with precision nicer still, the mind
He scans of ev'ry loco-motive kind;
Birds of all feather, beasts of ev'ry name,
That serve mankind, or shun them, wild or tame;
The looks and gestures of their griefs and fears
Have, all, articulation in his ears;
He spells them true by intuition's light,
And needs no glossary to set him right.   70
   This truth premis'd was needful as a text,
To win due credence to what follows next.
   Awhile they mus'd; surveying ev'ry face,
Thou hadst suppos'd them of superior race;
Their periwigs of wool, and fears combin'd,
Stamp'd on each countenance such marks of mind.
That sage they seem'd, as lawyers o'er a doubt,
Which, puzzling long, at last they puzzle out;
Or academic tutors, teaching youths,
Sure ne'er to want them, mathematic truths;   80
When thus a mutton, statelier than the rest,
A ram, the ewes and wethers, sad, address'd:
Friends! we have liv'd too long. I never heard
Sounds such as these, so worthy to be fear'd.
Could I believe, that winds for ages pent
In earth's dark womb have found at last a vent,

55

And from their prison-house below arise,
With all these hideous howlings to the skies,
I could be much compos'd, nor should appear
For such a cause to feel the slightest fear.   90
Yourselves have seen, what time the thunders roll'd
All night, me resting quiet in the fold.
Or heard we that tremendous bray alone,
I could expound the melancholy tone;
Should deem it by our old companion made,
The ass; for he, we know, has lately stray'd,
And being lost, perhaps, and wand'ring wide,
Might be suppos'd to clamour for a guide.
But ah! those dreadful yells what soul can hear,
That owns a carcase, and not quake for fear?   100
Daemons produce them doubtless, brazen-claw'd
And fang'd with brass the daemons are abroad;
I hold it, therefore, wisest and most fit,
That, life to save, we leap into the pit.
    Him answer'd then his loving mate and true,
But more discreet than he, a Cambrian ewe.
    How? leap into the pit our life to save?
To save our life leap all into the grave?
For can we find it less? Contemplate first
The depth how awful! falling there we burst;   110
Or should the brambles, interpos'd, our fall
In part abate, that happiness were small;
For with a race like theirs no chance I see
Of peace or ease to creatures clad as we.
Meantime, noise kills not. Be it Dapple's bray,
Or be it not, or be it whose it may,
And rush those other sounds, that seem by tongues
Of daemons utter'd, from whatever lungs,
Sounds are but sounds, and till the cause appear,
We have at least commodious standing here;   120

Come, fiend, come, fury, giant, monster, blast
From earth or hell, we can but plunge at last.
    While thus she spake, I fainter heard the peals,
For Reynard, close attended at his heels,
By panting dog, tir'd man, and spatter'd horse,
Through mere good fortune, took a diff'rent course.
The flock grew calm again, and I, the road
Following that led me to my own abode,
Much wonder'd that the silly sheep had found
Such cause of terror in an empty sound,   130
So sweet to huntsman, gentleman, and hound.

MORAL

Beware of desp'rate steps. The darkest day
(Live till to-morrow) will have pass'd away.

THE COLUBRIAD (1782)

Close by the threshold of a door nail'd fast
Three kittens sat: each kitten look'd aghast.
I, passing swift and inattentive by,
At the three kittens cast a careless eye;
Not much concern'd to know what they did there,
Not deeming kittens worth a poet's care.
But presently a loud and furious hiss
Caused me to stop, and to exclaim—what's this?
When, lo! upon the threshold met my view,
With head erect, and eyes of fiery hue,   10
A viper, long as Count de Grasse's queue.
Forth from his head his forked tongue he throws,
Darting it full against a kitten's nose;
Who having never seen in field or house
The like, sat still and silent, as a mouse:

57

Only, projecting with attention due
Her whisker'd face, she ask'd him—who are you?
On to the hall went I, with pace not slow,
But swift as lightning, for a long Dutch hoe;
With which well arm'd I hasten'd to the spot,   20
To find the viper. But I found him not,
And, turning up the leaves and shrubs around,
Found only, that he was not to be found.
But still the kittens, sitting as before,
Sat watching close the bottom of the door.
I hope—said I—the villain I would kill
Has slipt between the door and the door's sill;
And if I make despatch, and follow hard,
No doubt but I shall find him in the yard:—
For long ere now it should have been rehears'd,   30
'Twas in the garden that I found him first.
E'en there I found him; there the full-grown cat
His head with velvet paw did gently pat,
As curious as the kittens erst had been
To learn what this phenomenon might mean.
Fill'd with heroic ardour at the sight,
And fearing every moment he would bite,
And rob our household of our only cat
That was of age to combat with a rat,
With out-stretch'd hoe I slew him at the door,   40
And taught him NEVER TO COME THERE NO MORE .

EPITAPH ON A HARE (1783)

Here lies, whom hound did ne'er pursue,
   Nor swifter greyhound follow,
Whose foot ne'er tainted morning dew,
   Nor ear heard huntsman's hallo',

Old Tiney, surliest of his kind,
   Who, nurs'd with tender care,
And to domestic bounds confin'd,
   Was still a wild Jack-hare.   8

Though duly from my hand he took
   His pittance ev'ry night,
He did it with a jealous look,
   And, when he could, would bite.

His diet was of wheaten bread,
   And milk, and oats, and straw,
Thistles, or lettuces instead,
   With sand to scour his maw.   16

On twigs of hawthorn he regal'd,
   On pippins' russet peel;
And, when his juicy salads fail'd,
   Slic'd carrot pleas'd him well.

A Turkey carpet was his lawn,
   Whereon he lov'd to bound,
To skip and gambol like a fawn,
   And swing his rump around.   24

His frisking was at evening hours,
   For then he lost his fear;
But most before approaching show'rs,
   Or when a storm drew near.

Eight years and five round rolling moons
   He thus saw steal away,
Dozing out all his idle noons,
   And ev'ry night at play.   32

I kept him for his humour' sake,
    For he would oft beguile
My heart of thoughts that made it ache,
    And force me to a smile.

But now, beneath this walnut-shade
    He finds his long, last home,
And waits in snug concealment laid,
    'Till gentler Puss shall come.   40

He, still more aged, feels the shocks
    From which no care can save,
And, partner once of Tiney's box,
    Must soon partake his grave.

THE RETIRED CAT (1791)

A poet's cat, sedate and grave,
As poet well could wish to have,
Was much addicted to inquire
For nooks, to which she might retire,
And where, secure as mouse in chink,
She might repose, or sit and think.
I know not where she caught the trick—
Nature perhaps herself had cast her
In such a mould PHILOSOPHIQUE,
Or else she learn'd it of her master.   10
Sometimes ascending, debonair,
An apple tree or lofty pear,
Lodg'd with convenience in the fork,
She watched the gard'ner at his work;
Sometimes her ease and solace sought
In an old empty wat'ring pot,

There wanting nothing, save a fan,
To seem some nymph in her sedan,
Apparell'd in exactest sort,
And ready to be borne to court.   20
    But love of change it seems has place
Not only in our wiser race;
Cats also feel as well as we
That passion's force, and so did she.
Her climbing, she began to find,
Expos'd her too much to the wind,
And the old utensil of tin
Was cold and comfortless within:
She therefore wish'd instead of those,
Some place of more serene repose,   30
Where neither cold might come, nor air
Too rudely wanton with her hair,
And sought it in the likeliest mode
Within her master's snug abode.
    A draw'r,—it chanc'd, at bottom lin'd
With linen of the softest kind,
With such as merchants introduce
From India, for the ladies' use,—
A draw'r impending o'er the rest,
Half open in the topmost chest,   40
Of depth enough, and none to spare,
Invited her to slumber there.
Puss with delight beyond expression,
Survey'd the scene, and took possession.
Recumbent at her ease ere long,
And lull'd by her own hum-drum song,
She left the cares of life behind,
And slept as she would sleep her last,
When in came, housewifely inclin'd,
The chambermaid, and shut it fast.   50

By no malignity impell'd,
But all unconscious who it held.
    Awaken'd by the shock (cried puss)
Was ever cat attended thus!
The open draw'r was left, I see,
Merely to prove a nest for me,
For soon as I was well compos'd,
Then came the maid, and it was closed:
How smooth these 'kerchiefs, and how sweet,
O what a delicate retreat!   60
I will resign myself to rest
Till Sol, declining in the west,
Shall call to supper; when, no doubt,
Susan will come and let me out.
    The evening came, the sun descended,
And puss remain'd still unattended.
The night roll'd tardily away,
(With her indeed 'twas never day)
The sprightly morn her course renew'd,
The evening gray again ensued,   70
And puss came into mind no more
Than if entomb'd the day before.
With hunger pinch'd, and pinch'd for room,
She now presag'd approaching doom,
Not slept a single wink, or purr'd,
Conscious of jeopardy incurr'd.
    That night, by chance, the poet watching,
Heard an inexplicable scratching,
His noble heart went pit-a-pat,
And to himself he said—what's that?   80
He drew the curtain at the side,
And forth he peep'd, but nothing spied.
Yet, by his ear directed, guess'd
Something imprison'd in the chest,

And doubtful what, with prudent care,
Resolv'd it should continue there.
At length a voice, which well he knew,
A long and melancholy mew,
Saluting his poetic ears,
Consol'd him, and dispell'd his fears;   90
He left his bed, he trod the floor,
He 'gan in haste the draw'rs explore,
The lowest first, and without stop,
The rest in order to the top.
For 'tis a truth well known to most,
That whatsoever thing is lost,
We seek it, ere it come to light,
In ev'ry cranny but the right.
Forth skipp'd the cat; not now replete
As erst with airy self-conceit,   100
Nor in her own fond apprehension,
A theme for all the world's attention,
But modest, sober, cur'd of all
Her notions hyperbolical,
And wishing for a place to rest
Any thing rather than a chest:
Then stept the poet into bed,
With this reflexion in his head:

MORAL

Beware of too sublime a sense
Of your own worth and consequence!   110
The man who dreams himself so great,
And his importance of such weight,
That all around, in all that's done,
Must move and act for him alone,
Will learn, in school of tribulation,
The folly of his expectation.

TO THE NIGHTINGALE

Which the author heard sing on New-Year's Day, 1792

Whence is it, that amaz'd I hear
    From yonder wither'd spray,
This foremost morn of all the year,
    The melody of May?

And why, since thousands would be proud
    Of such a favour shewn,
Am I selected from the crowd,
    To witness it alone?   8

Sing'st thou, sweet Philomel, to me,
    For that I also long
Have practis'd in the groves like thee,
    Though not like thee in song?

Or sing'st thou rather under force
    Of some divine command,
Commission'd to presage a course
    Of happier days at hand?   16

Thrice welcome then! for many a long
    And joyless year have I,
As thou to-day, put forth my song
    Beneath a wintry sky.

But thee no wintry skies can harm,
    Who only need'st to sing,
To make ev'n January charm,
    And ev'ry season Spring.   24

5/30/09

64

ON A SPANIEL CALLED BEAU (1793)
Killing a Young Bird

A Spaniel, Beau, that fares like you,
    Well-fed, and at his ease,
Should wiser be, than to pursue
    Each trifle that he sees.

But you have kill'd a tiny bird,
    Which flew not till to-day,
Against my orders, whom you heard
    Forbidding you the prey.   8

Nor did you kill, what you might eat,
    And ease a doggish pain,
For him, though chas'd with furious heat,
    You left where he was slain.

Nor was he of the thievish sort,
    Or one whom blood allures,
But innocent was all his sport,
    Whom you have torn for yours.   16

My dog! what remedy remains,
    Since, teach you all I can,
I see you, after all my pains,
    So much resemble man!

BEAU'S REPLY (1793)

Sir! when I flew to seize the bird,
    In spite of your command,
A louder voice than yours I heard,
    And harder to withstand:

You cried—Forbear!—but in my breast
 A mightier cried—Proceed!
'Twas nature, Sir, whose strong behest
 Impell'd me to the deed.   8

Yet much as nature I respect,
 I ventur'd once to break
(As you perhaps may recollect)
 Her precept, for your sake;

And when your linnet, on a day,
 Passing his prison door,
Had flutter'd all his strength away,
 And panting press'd the floor,   16

Well knowing him a sacred thing,
 Not destin'd to my tooth,
I only kissed his ruffled wing,
 And lick'd the feathers smooth.

Let my obedience then excuse
 My disobedience now,
Nor some reproof yourself refuse
 From your aggriev'd Bow-wow!   24

If killing birds be such a crime,
 (Which I can hardly see)
What think you, Sir, of killing Time
 With verse address'd to me?

THE POPLAR-FIELD (1784)

The poplars are fell'd, farewell to the shade
And the whispering sound of the cool colonnade,
The winds play no longer, and sing in the leaves,
Nor Ouse on his bosom their image receives.

Twelve years have elaps'd since I last took a view
Of my favourite field and the bank where they grew,
And now in the grass behold they are laid,
And the tree is my seat that once lent me a shade.   8

The blackbird has fled to another retreat
Where the hazels afford him a screen from the heat,
And the scene where his melody charm'd me before,
Resounds with his sweet-flowing ditty no more.

My fugitive years are all hasting away,
And I must ere long lie as lowly as they,
With a turf on my breast, and a stone at my head,
Ere another such grove shall arise in its stead.   16

Tis a sight to engage me, if any thing can,
To muse on the perishing pleasures of man;
Though his life be a dream, his enjoyments, I see,
Have a being less durable even than he.

5/30/09

ODE TO APOLLO (1792)
On an ink-glass almost dried in the sun

Patron of all those luckless brains,
   That, to the wrong side leaning,
Indite much metre with much pains,
   And little or no meaning,

67

Ah, why, since oceans, rivers, streams
    That water all the nations,
Pay tribute to thy glorious beams,
    In constant exhalations,   8

Why, stooping from the noon of day,
    Too covetous of drink,
Apollo, hast thou stol'n away
    A poet's drop of ink?

Upborne into the viewless air
    It floats a vapour now,
Impell'd through regions dense and rare,
    By all the winds that blow.   16

Ordain'd, perhaps, ere summer flies,
    Combin'd with millions more,
To form an Iris in the skies,
    Though black and foul before.

Illustrious drop! and happy then
    Beyond the happiest lot,
Of all that ever pass'd my pen,
    So soon to be forgot!   24

Phœbus, if such be thy design,
    To place it in thy bow,
Give wit, that what is left may shine
    With equal grace below.

YARDLEY OAK (1791)

Survivor sole, and hardly such, of all
That once liv'd here thy brethren, at my birth
(Since which I number three-score winters past)
A shatter'd veteran, hollow-trunk'd perhaps
As now, and with excoriate forks deform,
Relicts of ages! Could a mind, imbued
With truth from heav'n, created thing adore,
I might with rev'rence kneel and worship thee.

    It seems idolatry with some excuse
When our fore-father Druids in their oaks   10
Imagin'd sanctity. The conscience yet
Unpurified by an authentic act
Of amnesty, the meed of blood divine,
Lov'd not the light, but gloomy into gloom
Of thickest shades, like Adam after taste
Of fruit proscrib'd, as to a refuge, fled.

    Thou wast a bauble once: a cup and ball,
Which babes might play with; and the thievish jay
Seeking her food, with ease might have purloin'd
The auburn nut that held thee, swallowing down   20
Thy yet close-folded latitude of boughs
And all thine embryo vastness, at a gulp.
But Fate thy growth decreed: autumnal rains
Beneath thy parent tree mellow'd the soil
Design'd thy cradle, and a skipping deer,
With pointed hoof dibbling the glebe, prepar'd
The soft receptacle in which secure
Thy rudiments should sleep the winter through.

    So Fancy dreams—Disprove it, if ye can,
Ye reas'ners broad awake, whose busy searce   30
Of argument, employ'd too oft amiss,
Sifts half the pleasures of short life away.

Thou fell'st mature, and in the loamy clod
Swelling, with vegetative force instinct
Didst burst thine egg, as theirs the fabled Twins
Now stars; two lobes, protruding, pair'd exact;
A leaf succeeded, and another leaf,
And all the elements thy puny growth
Fost'ring propitious, thou becam'st a twig.

    Who liv'd when thou wast such? Oh couldst thou speak,   40
As in Dodona once thy kindred trees
Oracular, I would not curious ask
The future, best unknown, but at thy mouth
Inquisitive, the less ambiguous past.

    By thee I might correct, erroneous oft,
The clock of history, facts and events
Timing more punctual, unrecorded facts
Recov'ring, and misstated setting right—
Desp'rate attempt, till trees shall speak again!

    Time made thee what thou wast—King of the woods;   50
And Time hath made thee what thou art—a cave
For owls to roost in. Once thy spreading boughs
O'erhung the champain; and the numerous flock
That graz'd it stood beneath that ample cope
Uncrowded, yet safe-sheltered from the storm.
No flock frequents thee now. Thou hast outliv'd
Thy popularity and art become
(Unless verse rescue thee awhile) a thing
Forgotten, as the foliage of thy youth.

    While thus through all the stages thou hast push'd   60
Of treeship, first a seedling hid in grass,
Then twig, then sapling, and, as century roll'd
Slow after century, a giant bulk
Of girth enormous, with moss-cushion'd root
Upheav'd above the soil, and sides imboss'd
With prominent wens globose, till at the last

The rottenness, which time is charg'd t' inflict
On other mighty ones, found also thee—
What exhibitions various hath the world
Witness'd of mutability in all   70
That we account most durable below!
Change is the diet, on which all subsist
Created changeable, and change at last
Destroys them.—Skies uncertain now the heat
Transmitting cloudless, and the solar beam
Now quenching in a boundless sea of clouds,—
Calm and alternate storm, moisture and drought,
Invigorate by turns the springs of life
In all that live, plant, animal, and man,
And in conclusion mar them. Nature's threads,   80
Fine passing thought, ev'n in her coarsest works,
Delight in agitation, yet sustain
The force, that agitates not unimpair'd,
But, worn by frequent impulse, to the cause
Of their best tone their dissolution owe.
    Thought cannot spend itself, comparing still
The great and little of thy lot, thy growth
From almost nullity into a state
Of matchless grandeur, and declension thence
Slow into such magnificent decay.   90
Time was, when, settling on thy leaf, a fly
Could shake thee to the root—and time has been
When tempests could not. At thy firmest age
Thou hadst within thy bole solid contents
That might have ribb'd the sides or plank'd the deck
Of some flagg'd admiral and tortuous arms,
The ship-wright's darling treasure, didst present
To the four-quarter'd winds, robust and bold,
Warp'd into tough knee-timber, many a load.
But the axe spar'd thee; in those thriftier days   100

71

Oaks fell not, hewn by thousands, to supply
The bottomless demands of contests wag'd
For senatorial honours. Thus to Time
The task was left to whittle thee away
With his sly scythe, whose ever-nibbling edge
Noiseless, an atom and an atom more
Disjoining from the rest, has, unobserv'd,
Achiev'd a labour, which had, far and wide,
(By man perform'd) made all the forest ring.

    Embowell'd now, and of thy ancient self   110
Possessing nought but the scoop'd rind, that seems
An huge throat calling to the clouds for drink,
Which it would give in riv'lets to thy root,
Thou temptest none, but rather much forbid'st
The feller's toil, which thou couldst ill requite.
Yet is thy root sincere, sound as the rock,
A quarry of stout spurs and knotted fangs,
Which, crook'd into a thousand whimsies, clasp
The stubborn soil, and hold thee still erect.

    So stands a kingdom, whose foundations yet   120
Fail not, in virtue and in wisdom laid,
Though all the superstructure, by the tooth
Pulveriz'd of venality, a shell
Stands now, and semblance only of itself.

    Thine arms have left thee. Winds have rent them off
Long since, and rovers of the forest wild
With bow and shaft have burnt them. Some have left
A splinter'd stump bleach'd to a snowy white;
And some memorial none where once they grew.
Yet life still lingers in thee, and puts forth   130
Proof not contemptible of what she can,
Even where death predominates. The spring
Thee finds not less alive to her sweet force
Than yonder upstarts of the neighbour wood,

So much thy juniors, who their birth receiv'd
Half a millennium since the date of thine.
    But since, although well qualified by age
To teach, no spirit dwells in thee, nor voice
May be expected from thee, seated here
On thy distorted root, with hearers none   140
Or prompter, save the scene, I will perform
Myself the oracle and will discourse
In my own ear such matter as I may.
Thou, like myself, hast stage by stage attain'd
Life's wintry bourn; thou, after many years,
I after few; but few or many prove
A span in retrospect; for I can touch
With my least finger's end my own decease
And with extended thumb my natal hour,
And hadst thou also skill in measurement   150
As I, the past would seem as short to thee.
Evil and few—said Jacob—at an age
Thrice mine, and few and evil, I may think
The Prediluvian race, whose buxom youth
Endured two centuries, accounted theirs.
'Shortliv'd as foliage is the race of man.
The wind shakes down the leaves, the budding grove
Soon teems with others, and in spring they grow.
So pass mankind. One generation meets
Its destin'd period, and a new succeeds.'   160
Such was the tender but undue complaint
Of the Mæonian in old time; for who
Would drawl out centuries in tedious strife
Severe with mental and corporeal ill
And would not rather chuse a shorter race
To glory, a few decads here below?
    One man alone, the Father of us all,
Drew not his life from woman; never gaz'd,

With mute unconsciousness of what he saw
On all around him; learn'd not by degrees, 170
Nor owed articulation to his ear;
But, moulded by his Maker into Man
At once, upstood intelligent, survey'd
All creatures, with precision understood
Their purport, uses, properties, assign'd
To each his name significant, and, fill'd
With love and wisdom, render'd back to heav'n
In praise harmonious the first air he drew.
He was excus'd the penalties of dull
Minority. No tutor charg'd his hand 180
With the thought-tracing quill, or task'd his mind
With problems; history, not wanted yet,
Lean'd on her elbow, watching Time, whose course,
Eventful, should supply her with a theme;
*   *   *   *   *   *

TO MARY (1793)

The twentieth year is well-nigh past,
Since first our sky was overcast;
Ah would that this might be the last!
> My Mary!

Thy spirits have a fainter flow,
I see thee daily weaker grow—
'Twas my distress that brought thee low,
> My Mary! 8

Thy needles, once a shining store,
For my sake restless heretofore,
Now rust disus'd, and shine no more,
> My Mary!

For though thou gladly wouldst fulfil
The same kind office for me still,
Thy sight now seconds not thy will,
                    My Mary!   16

But well thou play'd'st the housewife's part,
And all thy threads with magic art
Have wound themselves about this heart,
                    My Mary!

Thy indistinct expressions seem
Like language utter'd in a dream;
Yet me they charm, whate'er the theme,
                    My Mary!   24

Thy silver locks, once auburn bright,
Are still more lovely in my sight
Than golden beams of orient light,
                    My Mary!

For could I view nor them nor thee,
What sight worth seeing could I see?
The sun would rise in vain for me,
                    My Mary!   32

Partakers of the sad decline,
Thy hands their little force resign;
Yet, gently prest, press gently mine,
                    My Mary!

And then I feel that still I hold
A richer store ten thousandfold
Than misers fancy in their gold,
                    My Mary!   40

Such feebleness of limbs thou prov'st,
That now at every step thou mov'st
Upheld by two; yet still thou lov'st,

My Mary!

And still to love, though prest with ill,
In wintry age to feel no chill,
With me is to be lovely still,

My Mary!   48

But ah! by constant heed I know,
How oft the sadness that I show
Transforms thy smiles to looks of woe,

My Mary!

And should my future lot be cast
With much resemblance of the past,
Thy worn-out heart will break at last,

My Mary!   56

THE CASTAWAY (1799)

Obscurest night involv'd the sky,
    Th' Atlantic billows roar'd,
When such a destin'd wretch as I,
    Wash'd headlong from on board,
Of friends, of hope, of all bereft,
His floating home for ever left.   6

No braver chief could Albion boast
    Than he with whom he went,
Nor ever ship left Albion's coast,
    With warmer wishes sent.

He lov'd them both, but both in vain,
Nor him beheld, nor her again. 12

Not long beneath the whelming brine,
    Expert to swim, he lay;
Nor soon he felt his strength decline,
    Or courage die away;
But wag'd with death a lasting strife,   [wagged]
Supported by despair of life. 18

He shouted: nor his friends had fail'd
    To check the vessel's course,
But so the furious blast prevail'd,
    That, pitiless perforce,
They left their outcast mate behind,
And scudded still before the wind. 24

Some succour yet they could afford;
    And, such as storms allow,
The cask, the coop, the floated cord,
    Delay'd not to bestow.
But he (they knew) nor ship, nor shore,
Whate'er they gave, should visit more. 30

Nor, cruel as it seem'd, could he
    Their haste himself condemn,
Aware that flight, in such a sea,
    Alone could rescue them;
Yet bitter felt it still to die
Deserted, and his friends so nigh. 36

He long survives, who lives an hour
    In ocean, self-upheld;
And so long he, with unspent pow'r,

    His destiny repell'd;
And ever, as the minutes flew,
Entreated help, or cried—Adieu!   42

At length, his transient respite past,
   His comrades, who before
Had heard his voice in ev'ry blast,
   Could catch the sound no more.
For then, by toil subdued, he drank
The stifling wave, and then he sank.   48

No poet wept him: but the page
   Of narrative sincere,
That tells his name, his worth, his age,
   Is wet with Anson's tear.
And tears by bards or heroes shed
Alike immortalize the dead.   54

I therefore purpose not, or dream,
   Descanting on his fate,
To give the melancholy theme
   A more enduring date:
But misery still delights to trace
Its 'semblance in another's case.   60

No voice divine the storm allay'd,
   No light propitious shone;
When, snatch'd from all effectual aid,
   We perish'd, each alone:
But I beneath a rougher sea,
And whelm'd in deeper gulphs than he.   66

from THE TASK (1785)

from Book One

[144-209]
And witness, dear companion of my walks,
Whose arm this twentieth winter I perceive
Fast lock'd in mine, with pleasures such as love,
Confirm'd by long experience of thy worth
And well-tried virtues, could alone inspire—
Witness a joy which thou hast doubled long.
Thou know'st my praise of nature most sincere,   150
And that my raptures are not conjur'd up
To serve occasions of poetic pomp,
But genuine, and art partner of them all.
How oft upon yon eminence our pace
Has slacken'd to a pause, and we have born
The ruffling wind, scarce conscious that it blew,
While admiration, feeding at the eye,
And still unsated, dwelt upon the scene.
Thence with what pleasure have we just discern'd
The distant plough slow moving, and beside   160
His lab'ring team, that swerv'd not from the track,
The sturdy swain diminish'd to a boy!
Here Ouse, slow winding through a level plain
Of spacious meads with cattle sprinkled o'er,
Conducts the eye along its sinuous course
Delighted. There, fast-rooted in his bank,
Stand, never overlook'd, our fav'rite elms,
That screen the herdsman's solitary hut;
While far beyond, and overthwart the stream
That, as with molten glass, inlays the vale,   170
The sloping land recedes into the clouds;
Displaying on its varied side the grace

Of hedge-row beauties numberless, square tow'r,
Tall spire, from which the sound of cheerful bells
Just undulates upon the list'ning ear,
Groves, heaths, and smoking villages, remote.
Scenes must be beautiful, which, daily view'd,
Please daily, and whose novelty survives
Long knowledge and the scrutiny of years.
Praise justly due to those that I describe.   180
    Nor rural sights alone, but rural sounds,
Exhilarate the spirit, and restore
The tone of languid Nature. Mighty winds,
That sweep the skirt of some far-spreading wood
Of ancient growth, make music not unlike
The dash of ocean on his winding shore,
And lull the spirit while they fill the mind;
Unnumber'd branches waving in the blast,
And all their leaves fast flutt'ring, all at once.
Nor less composure waits upon the roar   190
Of distant floods, or on the softer voice
Of neighb'ring fountain, or of rills that slip
Through the cleft rock, and, chiming as they fall
Upon loose pebbles, lose themselves at length
In matted grass, that with a livelier green
Betrays the secret of their silent course.
Nature inanimate employs sweet sounds,
But animated nature sweeter still,
To sooth and satisfy the human ear.
Ten thousand warblers cheer the day, and one   200
The live-long night: nor these alone, whose notes
Nice finger'd art must emulate in vain,
But cawing rooks, and kites that swim sublime
In still repeated circles, screaming loud,
The jay, the pie, and ev'n the boding owl
That hails the rising moon, have charms for me.

Sounds inharmonious in themselves and harsh,
Yet heard in scenes where peace for ever reigns,
And only there, please highly for their sake.

[338-384]
Ye fallen avenues! once more I mourn
Your fate unmerited, once more rejoice
That yet a remnant of your race survives.   340
How airy and how light the graceful arch,
Yet awful as the consecrated roof
Re-echoing pious anthems! while beneath
The chequer'd earth seems restless as a flood
Brush'd by the wind. So sportive is the light
Shot through the boughs, it dances as they dance,
Shadow and sunshine intermingling quick,
And dark'ning and enlight'ning, as the leaves
Play wanton, ev'ry moment, ev'ry spot.
        And now, with nerves new-brac'd and spirits cheer'd,   350
We tread the wilderness, whose well-roll'd walks,
With curvature of slow and easy sweep—
Deception innocent—give ample space
To narrow bounds. The grove receives us next;
Between the upright shafts of whose tall elms
We may discern the thresher at his task.
Thump after thump resounds the constant flail,
That seems to swing uncertain, and yet falls
Full on the destin'd ear. Wide flies the chaff.
The rustling straw sends up a frequent mist   360
Of atoms, sparkling in the noon-day beam.
Come hither, ye that press your beds of down
And sleep not: see him sweating o'er his bread
Before he eats it.—'Tis the primal curse,
But soften'd into mercy; made the pledge
Of cheerful days, and nights without a groan.

81

By ceaseless action all that is subsists.
Constant rotation of th' unwearied wheel
That nature rides upon maintains her health,
Her beauty, her fertility. She dreads 370
An instant's pause, and lives but while she moves.
Its own revolvency upholds the world.
Winds from all quarters agitate the air,
And fit the limpid element for use,
Else noxious: oceans, rivers, lakes, and streams,
All feel the fresh'ning impulse, and are cleans'd
By restless undulation; ev'n the oak
Thrives by the rude concussion of the storm:
He seems indeed indignant, and to feel
Th' impression of the blast with proud disdain, 380
Frowning as if in his unconscious arm
He held the thunder: but the monarch owes
His firm stability to what he scorns—
More fixt below, the more disturb'd above.

[749-774]
    God made the country, and man made the town.
What wonder then that health and virtue, gifts 750
That can alone make sweet the bitter draught
That life holds out to all, should most abound
And least be threaten'd in the fields and groves?
Possess ye, therefore, ye, who, borne about
In chariots and sedans, know no fatigue
But that of idleness, and taste no scenes
But such as art contrives, possess ye still
Your element; there only can ye shine,
There only minds like your's can do no harm.
Our groves were planted to console at noon 760
The pensive wand'rer in their shades. At eve
The moon-beam, sliding softly in between

82

The sleeping leaves, is all the light they wish,
Birds warbling all the music. We can spare
The splendour of your lamps; they but eclipse
Our softer satellite. Your songs confound
Our more harmonious notes: the thrush departs
Scar'd, and th'offended nightingale is mute.
There is a public mischief in your mirth;
It plagues your country. Folly such as your's,   770
Grac'd with a sword, and worthier of a fan,
Has made, what enemies could ne'er have done,
Our arch of empire, stedfast but for you,
A mutilated structure, soon to fall.

from Book Two

[1-74]
Oh for a lodge in some vast wilderness,
Some boundless contiguity of shade,
Where rumour of oppression and deceit,
Of unsuccessful or successful war,
Might never reach me more. My ear is pain'd,
My soul is sick, with ev'ry day's report
Of wrong and outrage with which earth is fill'd.
There is no flesh in man's obdurate heart,
It does not feel for man; the nat'ral bond
Of brotherhood is sever'd as the flax   10
That falls asunder at the touch of fire.
He finds his fellow guilty of a skin
Not colour'd like his own; and, having pow'r
T' enforce the wrong, for such a worthy cause
Dooms and devotes him as his lawful prey.
Lands intersected by a narrow frith
Abhor each other. Mountains interpos'd

83

Make enemies of nations, who had else,
Like kindred drops, been mingled into one.
Thus man devotes his brother, and destroys; 20
And, worse than all, and most to be deplor'd,
As human nature's broadest, foulest blot,
Chains him, and tasks him, and exacts his sweat
With stripes, that mercy, with a bleeding heart,
Weeps when she sees inflicted on a beast.
Then what is man? And what man, seeing this,
And having human feelings, does not blush,
And hang his head, to think himself a man?
I would not have a slave to till my ground,
To carry me, to fan me while I sleep, 30
And tremble when I wake, for all the wealth
That sinews bought and sold have ever earn'd.
No: dear as freedom is, and in my heart's
Just estimation priz'd above all price,
I had much rather be myself the slave,
And wear the bonds, than fasten them on him.
We have no slaves at home.—Then why abroad?
And they themselves, once ferried o'er the wave
That parts us, are emancipate and loos'd.
Slaves cannot breathe in England; if their lungs 40
Receive our air, that moment they are free;
They touch our country, and their shackles fall.
That's noble, and bespeaks a nation proud
And jealous of the blessing. Spread it then,
And let it circulate through ev'ry vein
Of all your empire; that where Britain's pow'r
Is felt, mankind may feel her mercy too.
   Sure there is need of social intercourse,
Benevolence, and peace, and mutual aid,
Between the nations, in a world that seems 50
To toll the death-bell of its own decease,

And by the voice of all its elements
To preach the gen'ral doom. When were the winds
Let slip with such a warrant to destroy?
When did the waves so haughtily o'erleap
Their ancient barriers, deluging the dry?
Fires from beneath, and meteors from above,
Portentous, unexampled, unexplain'd,
Have kindled beacons in the skies; and th' old
And crazy earth has had her shaking fits   60
More frequent, and foregone her usual rest.
Is it a time to wrangle, when the props
And pillars of our planet seem to fail,
And Nature with a dim and sickly eye
To wait the close of all? But grant her end
More distant, and that prophecy demands
A longer respite, unaccomplish'd yet;
Still they are frowning signals, and bespeak
Displeasure in his breast who smites the earth
Or heals it, makes it languish or rejoice.   70
And 'tis but seemly, that, where all deserve
And stand expos'd by common peccancy
To what no few have felt, there should be peace,
And brethren in calamity should love.

from Book Three

[108-132]   (HI)

    I was a stricken deer, that left the herd
Long since; with many an arrow deep infixt
My panting side was charg'd, when I withdrew
To seek a tranquil death in distant shades.   110
There was I found by one who had himself
Been hurt by th' archers. In his side he bore,

85

And in his hands and feet, the cruel scars.
With gentle force soliciting the darts,
He drew them forth, and heal'd, and bade me live.
Since then, with few associates, in remote
And silent woods I wander, far from those
My former partners of the peopled scene;
With few associates, and not wishing more.   120
Here much I ruminate, as much I may,
With other views of men and manners now
Than once, and others of a life to come.
I see that all are wand'rers, gone astray
Each in his own delusions; they are lost
In chase of fancied happiness, still woo'd
And never won. Dream after dream ensues;
And still they dream that they shall still succeed.
And still are disappointed. Rings the world
With the vain stir. I sum up half mankind,   130
And add two thirds of the remaining half,
And find the total of their hopes and fears
Dreams, empty dreams.

[191-220]
    'Twere well, says one sage erudite, profound,
Terribly arch'd and aquiline his nose,
And overbuilt with most impending brows,
'Twere well, could you permit the world to live
As the world pleases. What's the world to you?—
Much. I was born of woman, and drew milk,
As sweet as charity, from human breasts.
I think, articulate, I laugh and weep,
And exercise all functions of a man.
How then should I and any man that lives   200
Be strangers to each other? Pierce my vein,
And take off the crimson stream meand'ring there,

And catechise it well, apply thy glass,
Search it, and prove now if it be not blood
Congenial with thine own: and, if it be,
What edge of subtlety canst thou suppose
Keen enough, wise and skilful as thou art,
To cut the link of brotherhood, by which
One common Maker bound me to the kind?
True; I am no proficient, I confess,   210
In arts like your's. I cannot call the swift
And perilous lightnings from the angry clouds,
And bid them hide themselves in earth beneath;
I cannot analyse the air, nor catch
The parallax of yonder luminous point,
That seems half quench'd in the immense abyss:
Such pow'rs I boast not—neither can I rest
A silent witness of the headlong rage
Or heedless folly by which thousands die,
Bone of my bone, and kindred souls to mine.   220

[261-265]
All flesh is grass, and all its glory fades
Like the fair flow'r dishevell'd in the wind;
Riches have wings, and grandeur is a dream:
The man we celebrate must find a tomb,
And we that worship him ignoble graves.

[320-351]
They love the country, and none else, who seek   320
For their own sake its silence and its shade.
Delights which who would leave, that has a heart
Susceptible to pity, or a mind
Cultur'd and capable of sober thought,
For all the savage din of the swift pack,
And clamours of the field?—Detested sport,

87

That owes its pleasures to another's pain;
That feeds upon the sobs and dying shrieks
Of harmless nature, dumb, but yet endu'd
With eloquence, that agonies inspire,   330
Of silent tears and heart-distending sighs!
Vain tears, alas, and sighs, that never find
A corresponding tone in jovial souls!
Well—one at least is safe. One shelter'd hare
Has never heard the sanguinary yell
Of cruel man, exulting in her woes.
Innocent partner of my peaceful home,
Whom ten long years' experience of my care
Has made at last familiar; she has lost
Much of her vigilant instinctive dread,   340
Not needful here, beneath a roof like mine.
Yes—thou may'st eat thy bread, and lick the hand
That feeds thee; thou may'st frolic on the floor
At evening, and at night retire secure
To thy straw couch, and slumber unalarm'd;
For I have gain'd thy confidence, have pledg'd
All that is human in me to protect
Thine unsuspecting gratitude and love.
If I survive thee I will dig thy grave;
And, when I place thee in it, sighing, say,   350
I knew at least one hare that had a friend.

from Book Four

[1-143]
Hark! 'tis the twanging horn! O'er yonder bridge,
That with its wearisome but needful length
Bestrides the wintry flood, in which the moon
Sees her unwrinkled face reflected bright;—

88

He comes, the herald of a noisy world,
With spatter'd boots, strapp'd waist, and frozen locks;
News from all nations lumb'ring at his back.
True to his charge, the close-pack'd load behind,
Yet careless what he brings, his one concern
Is to conduct it to the destin'd inn: 10
And, having dropp'd th' expected bag, pass on.
He whistles as he goes, light-hearted wretch,
Cold and yet cheerful: messenger of grief
Perhaps to thousands, and of joy to some;
To him indiff'rent whether grief or joy.
Houses in ashes, and the fall of stocks,
Births, deaths, and marriages, epistles wet
With tears, that trickled down the writer's cheeks
Fast as the periods from his fluent quill,
Or charg'd with am'rous sighs of absent swains,   20
Or nymphs responsive, equally affect
His horse and him, unconscious of them all.
But oh th' important budget! usher'd in
With such heart-shaking music, who can say
What are its tidings? have our troops awak'd?
Or do they still, as if with opium drugg'd,
Snore to the murmurs of th' Atlantic wave?
Is India free? and does she wear her plum'd
And jewell'd turban with a smile of peace,
Or do we grind her still? The grand debate,   30
The popular harangue, the tart reply,
The logic, and the wisdom, and the wit,
And the loud laugh—I long to know them all;
I burn to set th' imprison'd wranglers free,
And give them voice and utt'rance once again.
    Now stir the fire, and close the shutters fast,
Let fall the curtains, wheel the sofa round;
And, while the bubbling and loud-hissing urn

Throws up a steamy column, and the cups,
That cheer but not inebriate, wait on each, 40
So let us welcome peaceful ev'ning in.
Not such his ev'ning, who with shining face
Sweats in the crowded theatre, and, squeez'd
And bor'd with elbow-points through both his sides,
Out-scolds the ranting actor on the stage:
Nor his, who patient stands till his feet throb,
And his head thumps, to feed upon the breath
Of patriots, bursting with heroic rage,
Or placemen, all tranquillity and smiles.
This folio of four pages, happy work!
Which not ev'n critics criticise; that holds
Inquisitive attention, while I read,
Fast bound in chains of silence, which the fair,
Though eloquent themselves, yet fear to break;
What is it, but a map of busy life,
Its fluctuations, and its vast concerns?
Here runs the mountainous and craggy ridge
That tempts ambition. On the summit see
The seals of office glitter in his eyes;
He climbs, he pants, he grasps them! At his heels, 60
Close at his heels, a demagogue ascends,
And with a dext'rous jerk soon twists him down,
And wins them, but to lose them in his turn.
Here rills of oily eloquence in soft
Meanders lubricate the course they take;
The modest speaker is asham'd and griev'd
T' engross a moment's notice, and yet begs,
Begs a propitious ear for his poor thoughts,
However trivial all that he conceives.
Sweet bashfulness! It claims at least this praise, 70
The dearth of information and good sense
That it foretells us always comes to pass.

Cat'racts of declamation thunder here;
There forests of no meaning spread the page,
In which all comprehension wanders, lost;
While fields of pleasantry amuse us there
With merry descants on a nation's woes.
The rest appears a wilderness of strange
But gay confusion; roses for the cheeks,
And lilies for the brows of faded age,   80
Teeth for the toothless, ringlets for the bald,
Heav'n, earth, and ocean, plunder'd of their sweets,
Nectareous essences, Olympian dews,
Sermons, and city feasts, and fav'rite airs,
Ætherial journies, submarine exploits,
And Katterfelto, with his hair on end
At his own wonders, wond'ring for his bread.
      'Tis pleasant through the loop-holes of retreat
To peep at such a world; to see the stir
Of the great Babel, and not feel the crowd;   90
To hear the roar she sends through all her gates
At a safe distance, where the dying sound
Falls a soft murmur on th' uninjur'd ear.
Thus sitting, and surveying thus at ease
The globe and its concerns, I seem advanc'd
To some secure and more than mortal height,
That lib'rates and exempts me from them all.
It turns submitted to my view, turns round
With all its generations; I behold
The tumult, and am still. The sound of war   100
Has lost its terrors ere it reaches me;
Grieves, but alarms me not. I mourn the pride
And av'rice that make man a wolf to man;
Hear the faint echo of those brazen throats
By which he speaks the language of his heart,
And sigh, but never tremble at the sound.

He travels and expatiates, as the bee
From flow'r to flow'r, so he from land to land;
The manners, customs, policy of all
Pay contribution to the store he gleans;   110
He sucks intelligence in ev'ry clime,
And spreads the honey of his deep research
At his return—a rich repast for me.
He travels, and I too. I tread his deck,
Ascend his topmast, through his peering eyes
Discover countries, with a kindred heart
Suffer his woes, and share in his escapes;
While fancy, like the finger of a clock,
Runs the great circuit, and is still at home.
　　Oh Winter, ruler of th' inverted year,   120
Thy scatter'd hair with sleet like ashes fill'd,
Thy breath congeal'd upon thy lips, thy cheeks
Fring'd with a beard made white with other snows
Than those of age, thy forehead wrapt in clouds,
A leafless branch thy sceptre, and thy throne
A sliding car, indebted to no wheels,
But urg'd by storms along its slipp'ry way,
I love thee, all unlovely as thou seem'st,
And dreaded as thou art! Thou hold'st the sun
A pris'ner in the yet undawning east,   130
Short'ning his journey between morn and noon,
And hurrying him, impatient of his stay,
Down to the rosy west; but kindly still
Compensating his loss with added hours
Of social converse and instructive ease,
And gath'ring, at short notice, in one group
The family dispers'd, and fixing thought,
Not less dispers'd by day-light and its cares.
I crown thee king of intimate delights,
Fire-side enjoyments, home-born happiness,   140

And all the comforts that the lowly roof
Of undisturb'd retirement, and the hours
Of long uninterrupted ev'ning, know.

[243-332]
    Come, Ev'ning, once again, season of peace;
Return, sweet Ev'ning, and continue long!
Methinks I see thee in the streaky west,
With matron-step slow-moving, while the night
Treads on thy sweeping train; one hand employ'd
In letting fall the curtain of repose
On bird and beast, the other charg'd for man
With sweet oblivion of the cares of day: 250
Not sumptuously adorn'd, nor needing aid,
Like homely featur'd night, of clust'ring gems;
A star or two, just twinkling on thy brow,
Suffices thee; save that the moon is thine
No less than her's, not worn indeed on high
With ostentatious pageantry, but set
With modest grandeur in thy purple zone,
Resplendent less, but of an ampler round.
Come then, and thou shalt find thy vot'ry calm,
Or make me so. Composure is thy gift: 260
And, whether I devote thy gentle hours
To books, to music, or the poet's toil;
To weaving nets for bird-alluring fruit;
Or twining silken threads round iv'ry reels,
When they command whom man was born to please;
I slight thee not, but make thee welcome still.
    Just when our drawing-rooms begin to blaze
With lights, by clear reflection multiplied
From many a mirror, in which he of Gath,
Goliath, might have seen his giant bulk   270
Whole, without stooping, tow'ring crest and all,

93

My pleasures, too, begin. But me, perhaps,
The glowing hearth may satisfy awhile
With faint illumination, that uplifts
The shadow to the ceiling, there by fits
Dancing uncouthly to the quiv'ring flame.
Not undelightful is an hour to me
So spent in parlour twilight: such a gloom
Suits well the thoughtful or unthinking mind,
The mind contemplative, with some new theme   280
Pregnant, or indispos'd alike to all.
Laugh ye, who boast your more mercurial pow'rs,
That never feel a stupor, know no pause,
Nor need one, I am conscious, and confess,
Fearless, a soul that does not always think.
Me oft has fancy, ludicrous and wild,
Sooth'd with a waking dream of houses, tow'rs,
Trees, churches, and strange visages, express'd
In the red cinders, while with poring eye
I gaz'd, myself creating what I saw.   290
Nor less amus'd have I quiescent watch'd
The sooty films that play upon the bars,
Pendulous, and foreboding, in the view
Of superstition, prophesying still,
Though still deceiv'd, some stranger's near approach.
'Tis thus the understanding takes repose
In indolent vacuity of thought,
And sleeps and is refresh'd. Meanwhile the face
Conceals the mood lethargic with a mask
Of deep deliberation, as the man   300
Were task'd to his full strength, absorb'd and lost.
Thus oft, reclin'd at ease, I lose an hour
At ev'ning, till at length the freezing blast,
That sweeps the bolted shutter, summons home
The recollected pow'rs; and, snapping short

The glassy threads, with which the fancy weaves
Her brittle toys, restores me to myself.
How calm is my recess; and how the frost,
Raging abroad, and the rough wind, endear
The silence and the warmth enjoy'd within!
I saw the woods and fields, at close of day,
A variegated show; the meadows green,
Though faded; and the lands, where lately wav'd
The golden harvest, of a mellow brown,
Upturn'd so lately by the fearful share.
I saw far off the weedy fallows smile
With verdure not unprofitable, graz'd
By flocks, fast feeding, and selecting each
His fav'rite herb; while all the leafless groves,
That skirt th' horizon, wore a sable hue,   320
Scarce notic'd in the kindred dusk of eve.
To-morrow brings a change, a total change!
Which even now, though silently perform'd,
And slowly, and by most unfelt, the face
Of universal nature undergoes.
Fast falls a fleecy show'r: the downy flakes,
Descending, and with never-ceasing lapse,
Softly alighting upon all below,
Assimilate all objects. Earth receives
Gladly the thick'ning mantle; and the green   330
And tender blade, that fear'd the chilling blast,
Escapes unhurt beneath so warm a veil.

[780-801]
    Hail, therefore, patroness of health, and ease,   780
And contemplation, heart-consoling joys
And harmless pleasures, in the throng'd abode
Of multitudes unknown! hail, rural life!
Address himself who will to the pursuit

Of honours, or emolument, or fame;
I shall not add myself to such a chase,
Thwart his attempts, or envy his success.
Some must be great. Great offices will have
Great talents. And God gives to ev'ry man
The virtue, temper, understanding, taste,   790
That lifts him into life; and lets him fall
Just in the niche he was ordain'd to fill.
To the deliv'rer of an injur'd land
He gives a tongue t' enlarge upon, an heart
To feel, and courage to redress her wrongs;
To monarchs dignity; to judges sense;
To artists ingenuity and skill;
To me an unambitious mind, content
In the low vale of life, that early felt
A wish for ease and leisure, and ere long   800
Found here that leisure and that ease I wish'd.

from Book Five

[1-176]

'Tis morning; and the sun, with ruddy orb
Ascending, fires th' horizon: while the clouds,
That crowd away before the driving wind,
More ardent as the disk emerges more,
Resemble most some city in a blaze,
Seen through the leafless wood. His slanting ray
Slides ineffectual down the snowy vale,
And, tinging all with his own rosy hue,
From ev'ry herb and ev'ry spiry blade
Stretches a length of shadow o'er the field.   10
Mine, spindling into longitude immense,
In spite of gravity, and sage remark

96

That I myself am but a fleeting shade,
Provokes me to a smile. With eye askance
I view the muscular proportion'd limb
Transform'd to a lean shank. The shapeless pair,
As they design'd to mock me, at my side
Take step for step; and, as I near approach
The cottage, walk along the plaster'd wall,
Prepost'rous sight! the legs without the man.   20
The verdure of the plain lies buried deep
Beneath the dazzling deluge; and the bents,
And coarser grass, upspearing o'er the rest,
Of late unsightly and unseen, now shine
Conspicuous, and, in bright apparel clad
And fledg'd with icy feathers, nod superb.
The cattle mourn in corners where the fence
Screens them, and seem half petrified to sleep
In unrecumbent sadness. There they wait
Their wonted fodder, not like hung'ring man,   30
Fretful if unsupply'd; but silent, meek,
And patient of the slow-pac'd swain's delay.
He from the stack carves out th' accustom'd load,
Deep-plunging, and again deep-plunging oft,
His broad keen knife into the solid mass:
Smooth as a wall the upright remnant stands,
With such undeviating and even force
He severs it away: no needless care,
Lest storms should overset the leaning pile
Deciduous, or its own unbalanc'd weight.   40
Forth goes the woodman, leaving unconcern'd
The cheerful haunts of man; to wield the axe
And drive the wedge, in yonder forest drear,
From morn to eve his solitary task.
Shaggy, and lean, and shrewd, with pointed ears
And tail cropp'd short, half lurcher and half cur—

His dog attends him. Close behind his heel
Now creeps he slow; and now, with many a frisk
Wide-scamp'ring, snatches up the drifted snow
With iv'ry teeth, or ploughs it with his snout;   50
Then shakes his powder'd coat, and barks for joy.
Heedless of all his pranks, the sturdy churl
Moves right toward the mark; nor stops for aught,
But now and then with pressure of a thumb
T' adjust the fragrant charge of a short tube
That fumes beneath the nose; the trailing cloud
Streams far behind him, scenting all the air.
Now from the roost, or from the neighb'ring pale,
Where, diligent to catch the first faint gleam
Of smiling day, they gossip'd side by side,   60
Come trooping at the housewife's well-known call
The feather'd tribes domestic. Half on wing,
And half on foot, they brush the fleecy flood,
Conscious, and fearful of too deep a plunge.
The sparrows peep, and quit the shelt'ring eaves
To seize the fair occasion. Well they eye
The scatter'd grain; and, thievishly resolv'd
T' escape th' impending famine, often scar'd,
As oft return—a pert voracious kind.
Clean riddance quickly made, one only care   70
Remains to each—the search of sunny nook,
Or shed impervious to the blast. Resign'd
To sad necessity, the cock foregoes
His wonted strut and, wading at their head
With well-consider'd steps, seems to resent
His alter'd gait and stateliness retrench'd.
How find the myriads, that in summer cheer
The hills and vallies with their ceaseless songs,
Due sustenance, or where subsist they now?
Earth yields them nought: th' imprison'd worm is safe   80

Beneath the frozen clod; all seeds of herbs
Lie cover'd close; and berry-bearing thorns,
That feed the thrush, (whatever some suppose)
Afford the smaller minstrels no supply.
The long protracted rigour of the year
Thins all their num'rous flocks. In chinks and holes
Ten thousand seek an unmolested end,
As instinct prompts; self-buried ere they die.
The very rooks and daws forsake the fields,
Where neither grub, nor root, nor earth-nut, now
Repays their labour more; and, perch'd aloft   91
By the way-side, or stalking in the path,
Lean pensioners upon the trav'ler's track,
Pick up their nauseous dole, though sweet to them,
Of voided pulse or half-digested grain.
The streams are lost amid the splendid blank,
O'erwhelming all distinction. On the flood,
Indurated and fixt, the snowy weight
Lies undissolv'd; while silently beneath,
And unperceiv'd, the current steals away.   100
Not so where, scornful of a check, it leaps
The mill-dam, dashes on the restless wheel,
And wantons in the pebbly gulph below:
No frost can bind it there; its utmost force
Can but arrest the light and smoky mist
That in its fall the liquid sheet throws wide.
And see where it has hung th' embroider'd banks
With forms so various, that no pow'rs of art,
The pencil or the pen, may trace the scene!
Here glitt'ring turrets rise, upbearing high   110
(Fantastic misarrangement!) on the roof
Large growth of what may seem the sparkling trees
And shrubs of fairy land. The crystal drops
That trickle down the branches, fast congeal'd,

Shoot into pillars of pellucid length,
And prop the pile they but adorn'd before.
Here grotto within grotto safe defies
The sun-beam; there, emboss'd and fretted wild,
The growing wonder takes a thousand shapes
Capricious, in which fancy seeks in vain   120
The likeness of some object seen before.
Thus nature works as if to mock at art,
And in defiance of her rival pow'rs;
By these fortuitous and random strokes
Performing such inimitable feats
As she with all her rules can never reach.
Less worthy of applause, though more admir'd,
Because of novelty, the work of man,
Imperial mistress of the fur-clad Russ!
Thy most magnificent and mighty freak,
The wonder of the North. No forest fell
When thou wouldst build; no quarry sent its stores
T' enrich thy walls: but thou didst hew the floods,
And make thy marble of the glassy wave.
In such a palace Aristæus found
Cyrene, when he bore the plaintive tale
Of his lost bees to her maternal ear:
In such a palace poetry might place
The armory of winter; where his troops
The gloomy clouds, find weapons, arrowy sleet,   140
Skin-piercing volley, blossom-bruising hail,
And snow that often blinds the trav'ler's course,
And wraps him in an unexpected tomb.
Silently as a dream the fabric rose;—
No sound of hammer or of saw was there:
Ice upon ice, the well-adjusted parts
Were soon conjoin'd; nor other cement ask'd
Than water interfus'd to make them one.

Lamps gracefully dispos'd, and of all hues,
Illumin'd ev'ry side: a wat'ry light   150
Gleam'd through the clear transparency, that seem'd
Another moon new risen, or meteor fall'n
From heav'n to earth, of lambent flame serene.
So stood the brittle prodigy; though smooth
And slipp'ry the materials, yet frost-bound
Firm as a rock. Nor wanted aught within,
That royal residence might well befit,
For grandeur or for use. Long wavy wreaths
Of flow'rs, that fear'd no enemy but warmth,
Blush'd on the pannels. Mirror needed none   160
Where all was vitreous; but in order due
Convivial table and commodious seat
(What seem'd at least commodious seat) were there;
Sofa, and couch, and high-built throne august.
The same lubricity was found in all,
And all was moist to the warm touch; a scene
Of evanescent glory, once a stream,
And soon to glide into a stream again.
Alas! 'twas but a mortifying stroke
Of undesign'd severity, that glanc'd   170
(Made by a monarch) on her own estate,
On human grandeur and the courts of kings.
'Twas transient in its nature, as in show
'Twas durable: as worthless, as it seem'd
Intrinsically precious to the foot
Treach'rous and false; it smil'd, and it was cold.

[529-537]
All has its date below; the fatal hour
Was register'd in heav'n ere time began.   530
We turn to dust, and all our mightiest works
Die too: the deep foundations that we lay,

Time ploughs them up, and not a trace remains.
We build with what we deem eternal rock:
A distant age asks where the fabric stood;
And in the dust, sifted and search'd in vain,
The undiscoverable secret sleeps.

[688-703]
   Grace makes the slave a freeman. 'Tis a change
That turns to ridicule the turgid speech
And stately tone of moralists, who boast   690
As if, like him of fabulous renown,
They had indeed ability to smooth
The shag of savage nature, and were each
An Orpheus, and omnipotent in song:
But transformation of apostate man
From fool to wise, from earthly to divine,
Is work for Him that made him. He alone,
And he by means in philosophic eyes
Trivial and worthy of disdain, achieves
The wonder; humanizing what is brute   700
In the lost kind, extracting from the lips
Of asps their venom, overpow'ring strength
By weakness, and hostility by love.

[805-906]
   The soul that sees him, or receives sublim'd
New faculties, or learns at least t' employ
More worthily the pow'rs she own'd before;
Discerns in all things, what, with stupid gaze
Of ignorance, till then she overlook'd—
A ray of heav'nly light, gilding all forms   810
Terrestrial in the vast and the minute;
The unambiguous footsteps of the God
Who gives its lustre to an insect's wing,

And wheels his throne upon the rolling worlds.
Much conversant with heav'n, she often holds
With those fair ministers of light to man,
That fill the skies nightly with silent pomp,
Sweet conference: inquires what strains were they
With which heav'n rang, when ev'ry star, in haste
To gratulate the new-created earth   820
Sent forth a voice, and all the sons of God
Shouted for joy.—'Tell me, ye shining hosts,
That navigate a sea that knows no storms,
Beneath a vault unsullied with a cloud,
If from your elevation, whence ye view
Distinctly scenes invisible to man,
And systems of whose birth no tidings yet
Have reach'd this nether world, ye spy a race
Favour'd as our's; transgressors from the womb,
And hasting to a grave, yet doom'd to rise,   830
And to possess a brighter heav'n than your's?
As one who long detain'd on foreign shores
Pants to return, and when he sees afar
His country's weather-bleach'd and batter'd rocks,
From the green wave emerging, darts an eye
Radiant with joy towards the happy land;
So I with animated hopes behold,
And many an aching wish, your beamy fires,
That show like beacons in the blue abyss,
Ordain'd to guide th' embodied spirit home   840
From toilsome life to never-ending rest.
Love kindles as I gaze. I feel desires
That give assurance of their own success,
And that, infus'd from heav'n, must thither tend.'
   So reads the nature whom the lamp of truth
Illuminates. Thy lamp, mysterious word!
Which whoso sees no longer wanders lost,

103

With intellects bemaz'd in endless doubt,
But runs the road of wisdom. Thou hast built,
With means that were not till by thee employ'd,   850
Worlds that had never been hadst thou in strength
Been less, or less benevolent than strong.
They are thy witnesses, who speak thy pow'r
And goodness infinite, but speak in ears
That hear not, or receive not their report.
In vain thy creatures testify of thee
Till thou proclaim thyself. Their's is indeed
A teaching voice; but 'tis the praise of thine
That whom it teaches it makes prompt to learn,
And with the boon gives talents for its use.   860
Till thou art heard, imaginations vain
Possess the heart, and fables false as hell;
Yet deem'd oracular, lure down to death
The uninform'd and heedless souls of men.
We give to chance, blind chance, ourselves as blind,
The glory of thy work; which yet appears
Perfect and unimpeachable of blame,
Challenging human scrutiny, and prov'd
Then skilful most when most severely judg'd.
But chance is not, or is not where thou reign'st: 870
Thy providence forbids that fickle pow'r
(If power she be that works but to confound)
To mix her wild vagaries with thy laws.
Yet thus we dote, refusing while we can
Instruction, and inventing to ourselves
Gods such as guilt makes welcome; gods that sleep,
Or disregard our follies, or that sit
Amus'd spectators of this bustling stage.
Thee we reject, unable to abide
Thy purity, till pure as thou art pure;   880
Made such by thee, we love thee for that cause

For which we shunn'd and hated thee before.
Then we are free. Then liberty, like day,
Breaks on the soul, and by a flash from heav'n
Fires all the faculties with glorious joy.
A voice is heard that mortal ears hear not
Till thou hast touch'd them; 'tis the voice of song—
A loud hosanna sent from all thy works;
Which he that hears it with a shout repeats,
And adds his rapture to the gen'ral praise.   890
In that blest moment Nature, throwing wide
Her veil opaque, discloses with a smile
The author of her beauties, who, retir'd
Behind his own creation, works unseen
By the impure, and hears his power denied.
Thou art the source and centre of all minds,
Their only point of rest, eternal Word!
From thee departing, they are lost, and rove
At random, without honour, hope, or peace.
From thee is all that sooths the life of man,   900
His high endeavour, and his glad success,
His strength to suffer, and his will to serve.
But oh thou bounteous giver of all good,
Thou art of all thy gifts thyself the crown!
Give what thou canst, without thee we are poor;
And with thee rich, take what thou wilt away.

from Book Six

[1-14]
There is in souls a sympathy with sounds;
And, as the mind is pitch'd, the ear is pleas'd
With melting airs, or martial, brisk, or grave:
Some chord in unison with what we hear

105

Is touch'd within us, and the heart replies.
How soft the music of those village bells,
Falling at intervals upon the ear
In cadence sweet, now dying all away,
Now pealing loud again, and louder still,
Clear and sonorous, as the gale comes on!　　　　　　　10
With easy force it opens all the cells
Where mem'ry slept. Wherever I have heard
A kindred melody, the scene recurs,
And with it all its pleasures and its pains.

[57-87]
　　The night was winter in his roughest mood;
The morning sharp and clear. But now at noon
Upon the southern side of the slant hills,
And where the woods fence off the northern blast,　　　60
The season smiles, resigning all its rage,
And has the warmth of May. The vault is blue
Without a cloud, and white without a speck
The dazzling splendour of the scene below.
Again the harmony comes o'er the vale;
And through the trees I view th' embattled tow'r
Whence all the music. I again perceive
The soothing influence of the wafted strains,
And settle in soft musings as I tread
The walk, still verdant, under oaks and elms,　　　　　70
Whose outspread branches overarch the glade.
The roof, though moveable through all its length
As the wind sways it, has yet well suffic'd,
And, intercepting in their silent fall
The frequent flakes, has kept a path for me.
No noise is here, or none that hinders thought.
The redbreast warbles still, but is content
With slender notes, and more than half suppress'd:

Pleas'd with his solitude, and flitting light
From spray to spray, where'er he rests he shakes   80
From many a twig the pendant drops of ice,
That tinkle in the wither'd leaves below.
Stillness, accompanied with sounds so soft,
Charms more than silence. Meditation here
May think down hours to moments. Here the heart
May give an useful lesson to the head,
And learning wiser grow without his books.

[132-261]
All we behold is miracle; but, seen
So duly, all is miracle in vain.
Where now the vital energy that mov'd,
While summer was, the pure and subtle lymph
Through th' imperceptible meand'ring veins
Of leaf and flow'r? It sleeps; and th' icy touch
Of unprolific winter has impress'd
A cold stagnation on th' intestine tide.
But let the months go round, a few short months,   140
And all shall be restor'd. These naked shoots,
Barren as lances, among which the wind
Makes wintry music, sighing as it goes,
Shall put their graceful foliage on again,
And, more aspiring, and with ampler spread,
Shall boast new charms, and more than they have lost.
Then, each in its peculiar honours clad,
Shall publish, even to the distant eye,
Its family and tribe. Laburnum, rich
In streaming gold; syringa, iv'ry pure;   150
The scentless and the scented rose; this red
And of an humbler growth, the other tall,
And throwing up into the darkest gloom
Of neighb'ring cypress, or more sable yew,

107

Her silver globes, light as the foamy surf
That the wind severs from the broken wave;
The lilac, various in array, now white,
Now sanguine, and her beauteous head now set
With purples spikes pyramidal, as if,
Studious of ornament, yet unresolv'd   160
Which hue she most approv'd, she chose them all;
Copious of flow'rs the woodbine, pale and wan,
But well compensating her sickly looks
With never-cloying odours, early and late;
Hypericum, all bloom, so thick a swarm
Of flow'rs, like flies clothing her slender rods,
That scarce a leaf appears; mezerion, too,
Though leafless, well attir'd, and thick beset
With blushing wreaths, investing ev'ry spray;
Althæa with the purple eye; the broom,   170
Yellow and bright, as bullion unalloy'd,
Her blossoms, and, luxuriant above all,
The jasmine, throwing wide her elegant sweets,
The deep dark green of whose unvarnish'd leaf
Makes more conspicuous, and illumines more
The bright profusion of her scatter'd stars.—
These have been, and these shall be in their day;
And all this uniform, uncolour'd scene,
Shall be dismantled of its fleecy load,
And flush into variety again.   180
From dearth to plenty, and from death to life,
Is Nature's progress when she lectures man
In heav'nly truth; evincing, as she makes
The grand transition, that there lives and works
A soul in all things, and that soul is God.
The beauties of the wilderness are his,
That make so gay the solitary place
Where no eye sees them. And the fairer forms

That cultivation glories in, are his.
He sets the bright procession on its way,   190
And marshals all the order of the year;
He marks the bounds which winter may not pass,
And blunts his pointed fury; in its case,
Russet and rude, folds up the tender germ,
Uninjur'd, with inimitable art;
And, ere one flow'ry season fades and dies,
Designs the blooming wonders of the next.
   Some say that, in the origin of things,
When all creation started into birth,
The infant elements receiv'd a law,   200
From which they swerve not since. That under force
Of that controuling ordinance they move,
And need not his immediate hand, who first
Prescrib'd their course, to regulate it now.
Thus dream they, and contrive to save a God
Th' incumbrance of his own concerns, and spare
The great Artificer of all that moves
The stress of a continual act, the pain
Of unremitted vigilance and care,
As too laborious and severe a task.   210
So man, the moth, is not afraid, it seems,
To span omnipotence, and measure might
That knows no measure, by the scanty rule
And standard of his own, that is to-day,
And is not ere to-morrow's sun go down!
But how should matter occupy a charge
Dull as it is, and satisfy a law
So vast in its demands, unless impell'd
To ceaseless service by a ceaseless force,
And under pressure of some conscious cause?   220
The Lord of all, himself through all diffus'd,
Sustains, and is the life of all that lives.

Nature is but a name for an effect,
Whose cause is God. He feeds the secret fire
By which the mighty process is maintained,
Who sleeps not, is not weary; in whose sight
Slow circling ages are as transient days;
Whose work is without labour; whose designs
No flaw deforms, no difficulty thwarts;
And whose beneficence no charge exhausts.   230
Him blind antiquity profan'd, not serv'd,
With self-taught rites, and under various names,
Female and male, Pomona, Pales, Pan,
And Flora, and Vertumnus; peopling earth
With tutelary goddesses and gods
That were not; and commending, as they would,
To each some province, garden, field, or grove.
But all are under one. One spirit—His
Who wore the platted thorns with bleeding brows—
Rules universal nature. Not a flow'r   240
But shows some touch, in freckle, streak or stain,
Of his unrivall'd pencil. He inspires
Their balmy odours, and imparts their hues,
And bathes their eyes with nectar, and includes,
In grains as countless as the sea-side sands,
The forms with which he sprinkles all the earth.
Happy who walks with him! whom what he finds
Of flavour or of scent in fruit or flow'r,
Or what he views of beautiful or grand
In nature, from the broad majestic oak   250
To the green blade that twinkles in the sun,
Prompts with remembrance of a present God!
His presence, who made all so fair, perceiv'd,
Makes all still fairer. As with him no scene
Is dreary, so with him all seasons please.
Though winter had been none, had man been true,

And earth be punish'd for its tenant's sake,
Yet not in vengeance; as this smiling sky,
So soon succeeding such an angry night,
And these dissolving snows, and this clear stream   260
Recov'ring fast its liquid music, prove.

[295-320]
    Here, unmolested, through whatever sign
The sun proceeds, I wander. Neither mist,
Nor freezing sky nor sultry, checking me,
Nor stranger intermeddling with my joy.
Ev'n in the spring and play-time of the year,
That calls th' unwonted villager abroad   300
With all her little ones, a sportive train,
To gather king-cups in the yellow mead,
And prink their hair with daisies, or to pick
A cheap but wholesome sallad from the brook,
These shades are all my own. The tim'rous hare,
Grown so familiar with her frequent guest,
Scarce shuns me; and the stock-dove, unalarm'd,
Sits cooing in the pine-tree, nor suspends
His long love-ditty for my near approach.
Drawn from his refuge in some lonely elm   310
That age or injury has hollow'd deep,
Where, on his bed of wood and matted leaves,
He has outslept the winter, ventures forth
To frisk awhile, and bask in the warm sun,
The squirrel, flippant, pert, and full of play:
He sees me, and at once, swift as a bird,
Ascends the neighb'ring beech; where whisks his brush,
And perks his ears, and stamps and scolds aloud,
With all the prettiness of feign'd alarm,
And anger insignificantly fierce.   320

Oh scenes surpassing fable, and yet true,
Scenes of accomplish'd bliss! which who can see,   760
Though but in distant prospect, and not feel
His soul refresh'd with foretaste of the joy?
Rivers of gladness water all the earth,
And clothe all climes with beauty; the reproach
Of barrenness is past. The fruitful field
Laughs with abundance; and the land, once lean,
Or fertile only in its own disgrace,
Exults to see its thistly curse repeal'd.
The various seasons woven into one,
And that one season an eternal spring,   770
The garden fears no blight, and needs no fence,
For there is none to covet, all are full.
The lion, and the libbard, and the bear
Graze with the fearless flocks all bask at noon
Together, or all gambol in the shade
Of the same grove, and drink one common stream.
Antipathies are none. No foe to man
Lurks in the serpent now: the mother sees,
And smiles to see, her infant's playful hand
Stretch'd forth to dally with the crested worm,   780
To stroke his azure neck, or to receive
The lambent homage of his arrowy tongue.
All creatures worship man, and all mankind
One Lord, one Father. Error has no place:
That creeping pestilence is driv'n away;
The breath of heav'n has chas'd it. In the heart
No passion touches a discordant string,
But all is harmony and love. Disease
Is not: the pure and uncontam'nate blood
Holds its due course, nor fears the frost of age.   790
One song employs all nations; and all cry,

'Worthy the Lamb, for he was slain for us!'
The dwellers in the vales and on the rocks
Shout to each other, and the mountain tops
From distant mountains catch the flying joy;
Till, nation after nation taught the strain,
Earth rolls the rapturous hosanna round.
Behold the measure of the promise fill'd;
See Salem built, the labour of a God!
Bright as a sun the sacred city shines;   800
All kingdoms and all princes of the earth
Flock to that light; the glory of all lands
Flows into her; unbounded is her joy,
And endless her increase.

[906-914]
   He is the happy man, whose life ev'n now
Shows somewhat of that happier life to come;
Who, doom'd to an obscure but tranquil state,
Is pleas'd with it, and, were he free to choose,
Would make his fate his choice; whom peace, the fruit   910
Of virtue, and whom virtue, fruit of faith,
Prepare for happiness; bespeak him one
Content indeed to sojourn while he must
Below the skies, but having there his home.

[995-1005]
So life glides smoothly and by stealth away,
More golden than that age of fabled gold
Renown'd in ancient song; not vex'd with care
Or stain'd with guilt, beneficent, approv'd
Of God and man, and peaceful in its end.
So glide my life away! and so at last,   1000
My share of duties decently fulfill'd,
May some disease, not tardy to perform

113

Its destin'd office, yet with gentle stroke,
Dismiss me, weary, to a safe retreat,
Beneath the turf that I have often trod.

NOTES

(C) indicates Cowper's original footnote

Page 23: 'On the Receipt of My Mother's Picture'
The miniature—the only one in existence—was sent to Cowper by his
cousin Anne Bodham, daughter of the Rev. Roger Donne.

> The world could not have furnished you with a present so accept-
> able to me, as the picture which you have so kindly sent me. I
> received it the night before last, and viewed it with a trepidation
> of nerves and spirits somewhat akin to what I should have felt,
> had the dear original presented herself to my embraces. . . . She
> died when I completed my sixth year; yet I remember her well,
> and am an ocular witness of the great fidelity of the copy. I
> remember, too, a multitude of maternal tendernesses which I
> received from her, and which have endeared her memory to me
> beyond expression. (Letter to Mrs Bodham, 27 February 1790)

l. 46 *Where once we dwelt*, Berkhamstead rectory.
l. 97 Garth (C). Sir Samuel Garth, *The Dispensary* (1699), Canto
III, l. 226: 'Where billows never break, nor tempests roar'.

Page 26: 'Conversation'
See St Luke, xxiv, 13-22.

Page 27: 'Retirement'

> My view in choosing this subject is to direct to the proper use of the
> opportunities it affords for the cultivation of a man's best interests;
> to censure the vices and the follies which people carry with them
> into their retreats, where they make no other use of their leisure
> than to gratify themselves with the indulgence of their favourite
> appetites, and to pay themselves, by a life of pleasure, for a life of
> business. (Letter to John Newton, 25 August 1781)

Page 38: 'Alexander Selkirk'
Alexander Selkirk was born in Fifeshire in 1676. He took to sea
after a family quarrel and eventually landed up on the island of

Juan Fernandez. His adventures are said to have furnished Defoe with material for *Robinson Crusoe*.

Page 40: 'On the Loss of the Royal George'
The *Royal George*, 108 guns, was the pride of the fleet. She was undergoing repairs off Spithead on 29 August 1782 when the sudden squall hit and 'overset' her.

Page 41: 'John Gilpin'
Cowper heard this tale from Lady Austen, one evening in October, 1782. He wrote the entire ballad that night. When published—first, anonymously, in *The Public Advertiser* (November 1782)—it proved extremely popular. There followed John Gilpin recitations, John Gilpin chapbooks, and innumerable 'sequels' and prints of the comically helpless rider.

> I little thought when I was writing the history of John Gilpin, that he would appear in print—I intended to laugh, and to make two or three others laugh, of whom you were one. But now all the world laughs . . . (Letter to William Unwin, 18 November 1782)

l. 3 *train-band*, a citizen's militia.

l. 178 *merry pin,* merry humour.

Page 51: 'On the Death of Mrs Throckmorton's Bulfinch'
Weston has not been without its tragedies since you left us; Mrs Throckmorton's piping bullfinch has been eaten by a rat, and the villain left nothing but its beak. It will be a wonder if this event does not at some convenient time employ my versifying passion. (Letter to Samuel Rose, 11 November 1788)

The Throckmortons were close friends of Cowper. They lived in the village of Weston Underwood, near Olney.

ll. 62ff. Orpheus, the legendary poet, was torn to pieces by the crazed votaries of Bacchus. His head floated down the Hebrus, still speaking.

116

Page 57: 'The Colubriad'

See letter to William Unwin, 3 August 1782.

The mock-heroic title derives from *coluber*, the Latin word for snake.
l. 11 *Count de Grasse*, a French admiral: caricaturists poked fun at
his long 'queue', or wig-tail.

Page 58: 'Epitaph on a Hare'

Cowper's prose account of his three pet hares—reprinted in Mil-
ford's edition (pp. 669-671)—first appeared in *The Gentleman's
Magazine* for June 1784. This epitaph was published six months
later as a sequel.

Page 64: 'To the Nightingale'

You talk of primroses that you pulled on Candlemas Day; but
what think you of me who heard a nightingale on New Year's
Day? Perhaps I am the only man in England who can boast of
such good fortune . . . (Letter to John Johnson, 11 March 1792)

Page 67: 'The Poplar Field'

There was, indeed, some time since, in neighbouring parish called
Lavendon, a field, one side of which formed a terrace, and the
other was planted with poplars, at whose foot ran the Ouse, that
I used to account a little paradise: but the poplars have been
felled, and the scene has suffered so much by the loss, that
though still in point of prospect beautiful, it has not charms suf-
ficient to attract me now. (Letter to Lady Hesketh, 1 May 1786)

Page 69: 'Yardley Oak'

See Cowper's letter to Lady Hesketh, 13 September 1788.

The oak stood in Yardley Chase, near Olney. The poem was not
completed.

Page 74: 'To Mary'

l. 2 A reference to Cowper's severe bout of depression in 1773.

Page 76: 'The Castaway'

The poem is based on an incident in Richard Walter's *A Voyage Round the World by . . . George Anson* (1748). Anson's ship, *The Centurion*, was rounding Cape Horn in a storm on 24 March 1741, when a member of the crew, one of the 'ablest seamen', was washed overboard.

> . . . and notwithstanding the prodigious agitation of the waves, we perceived that he swam very strong, and it was with the utmost concern that we found ourselves incapable of assisting him; and we were the more grieved at his unhappy fate, since we lost sight of him struggling with the waves, and conceived from the manner in which he swam, that he might continue sensible for a considerable time longer, of the horror attending his irretrievable situation. (1798 edition, Book I, Chapter 8)

'The Task'
Page 79: *from Book One* 'The Sofa'

l. 144 *dear companion*, Mary Unwin.

l. 173 *square tow'r*, Clifton Reynes.

l. 174 *Tall spire*, Olney.

Page 83: *from Book Two* 'The Time-Piece'

Cowper explained the title in a letter to John Newton, 13 December 1784: 'The book to which it belongs is intended to strike the hour that gives notice of approaching judgment . . .'.

l. 1 Jeremiah ix, 2.

l. 53 Alluding to the late calamities at Jamaica (C). The island had been hit by severe hurricanes.

l. 64 Alluding to the fog that covered both Europe and Asia during the summer of 1783 (C). The fog caused widespread alarm. See letters to John Newton, 13 and 17 June 1783.

Page 85: *from Book Three* 'The Garden'

l. 261 Isiaiah xl, 6.

l. 263 Proverbs xxiii, 5.

l. 334 *one hare*, Cowper's pet hare, Puss. After the poet's death the following memorandum was found amongst his papers:

Tuesday, March 9, 1786—This day died poor Puss, aged eleven years eleven months. She died between twelve and one at noon, of mere old age, and apparently without pain.

Page 88: *from Book Four* 'The Winter Evening'

l. 1 *yonder bridge*, Olney bridge.

l. 2 *needful length*, the Ouse often floods.

l. 27 The reference is to the American war.

l. 85 *Aetherial journies, submarine exploits*, ballooning and the use of diving bells.

l. 86 Katterfelto was a well-known London quack, who began his advertisements with the words, 'Wonders! Wonders! Wonders!'

Page 96: *from Book Five* 'The Winter Morning Walk'

l. 129ff. The ice-palace of St Petersburg was constructed by the Tsarina Anna in the winter of 1740. The blocks were cut from the Neva. It survived from January till March.

ll. 135-7 Aristæus, son of Apollo and a water nymph named Cyrene, was the Greek god of beekeeping. The Dryads deprived him of his bees as a punishment for his part in the death of Eurydice.

Page 105: *from Book Six* 'The Winter Walk at Noon'

l. 66 *th'embattled tow'r*, of Emberton Church.

l. 298 Proverbs xiv, 10.

l. 768 cf. Genesis iii, 17-18.

l. 773 *libbard* (OE), leopard.

l. 792 Isaac Watts, 'Come let us join our cheerful songs', ll. 7-8.

Fyfield*Books*

Two millennia of essential classics

The extensive Fyfield*Books* list includes

For more information, including a full list of Fyfield*Books* and a contents list for each title, and details of how to order the books in the UK, visit the Fyfield website at www.fyfieldbooks.co.uk or email info@fyfieldbooks.co.uk. For information about Fyfield*Books* available in the United States and Canada, visit the Routledge website at www.routledge-ny.com.